The Canadian City

The Canadian City

ST. JOHN'S to VICTORIA

A Critical Commentary

Text and Illustrations by
Roger Kemble

Harvest House
<small>MONTREAL</small>

Deposited in the Bibliothèque nationale of Québec, 4th Quarter, 1989.

Typography and Cover: Naoto Kondo

Printed in Canada

First Harvest House Edition

For information address:
Harvest House Ltd., 1200 Atwater Ave., Suite #1
Montreal, Canada H3Z 1X4

Canadian Cataloguing in Publication Data

Kemble, Roger, 1929-
The Canadian city: St. John's to Victoria: a critical commentary

Includes bibliographical references.

ISBN 0-88772-222-9

1. Sociology, Urban—Canada. 2. Cities and towns—Canada.
3. City planning—Canada. I. Title.

HT127.K44 1989   307.7′6′0971   C89-090386-7

Dedicated to
the memory of
Gerald
and
Gladys Kemble

Contents

Preface

In 1987 I visited almost every major city in the country. This book is a commentary on what I found. For weeks I wandered, clicked my camera, surveyed, took elevations, sketched, talked to people and just people watched. All told, I surveyed sixty-four major urban spaces in all kinds of weather from −27°C below in Montreal to the humidity of summer in the Ottawa Valley. Limited resources and my diminishing energy confined my work to downtown, commonly known as the central business district, or very close.

What I saw was both invigorating and perplexing. Invigorating, because Canadian cities are vigorous, exciting, energetic going concerns; perplexing, because there is amidst such abundance a squalor and chaos that is hard to endure on a sustained basis. Accordingly, some of my opinions will run counter to intrenched interests.

I have directed deserved and pointed criticism towards many sacred cows. For thirty years we Canadian architects and planners have had a free ride and I personally (and many of the public agree) am not satisfied with the results. Where I have been critical of the built urban environment, I have balanced that criticism by articulating reasonable remedial processes to help heal the self-inflicted urban wounds.

I challenge my own planning and architectural professions. If we do not awaken from our comfortable myopia we will continue to languish irrelevantly. I hope this book will be an awakening. Indeed, its very purpose is to dislodge the current self-congratulatory smug condition and redefine the national dialogue on the subject.

When I returned, late in life, to the School of Community and Regional Planning at the University of British Columbia to take my master's degree, I was surprised to find virtually no literature on the design of Canadian cities. The bibliography is sparse. What literature there is comes mainly from the United Kingdom or the United States and of course their books are replete with the baggage and prejudices of those respective countries.

In fact, what literature exists comes from sources more intent on obscuring the real condition of city design, feel good stuff, mostly. So many people and institutions have a vested interest in the status quo, genuine criticism is muted. So upon graduation I resolved to take a look, follow up on some vague ideas taking into account my experiences both practical and academic, not realizing this book in its present form would materialize.

Canadian cities are to all intents and purposes uninhabitable. We can no longer afford to live downtown and the environment is so hostile we may not wish to do so. Visual chaos, noise, discord makes the environment stressful. This statement may come as a surprise. Still, it is my belief we have, of necessity, inured ourselves to the impact and consequences the discord has on our well-being.

If the city is to be the exclusive domain of bank towers, offices and expensive condominiums, ultimately it will atrophy. The city must be returned to the people who are building and paying for it.

Some city councils recognize this and wish to make amends. Much of the effort so far is just talk. The current crop of politicians gaze starry-eyed into the future and declare, as we lurch from one crisis to another, the market will take care of everything. Some hope!

Recently the mayor of Toronto exhumed the forgotten cry for the livable city. The subject of the livable in the city is vast. Accordingly, *The Canadian City* addresses a neglected, yet vital, part of the livable city — public urban space as an amenity for living and working downtown. It attempts to put forward the notion that public urban space is a direct outcome of a shared vision of urban space.

Politics and economics are far more potent elements in proscribing our lives, of course, than space, but if once we could get our act together the amenity of public urban space in the city could truly come into its own.

I cannot lay claim to have written the definitive resource on city design or public urban spaces for I am primarily a practitioner. Indeed, urban scholarship is currently largely devoted to the city as history and nostalgia. I have avoided historic and scholarly reference in the text, unless a few anecdotal remarks illuminate my point. Urban history and theory is well covered in other publications, a number of which are cited in the references at the end of this book.

The reader should not be intimidated, however, by what looks to be at first glance heavy theory. There are no earth-shattering new revelations here. What is stated are ideas to open up discussion that has unjustifiably (considering the importance urban space has in all our lives) remained dormant. I want elected representatives, administrators, developers and the general public to pick up this book, browse through it, enjoy the illustrations and ruminate on the contents.

The subject, as I mentioned in the previous paragraphs, is too large and elusive for any one author to even try the definitive treatise. Therefore, I have identified one small part of the urban environment that describes the condition of the city as it stands today — the appearance and commodious disposition of Canadian public urban spaces.

Public urban space and the architecture it comprises are the media of communication of the city. The medium of urban space describes to us the current state of the city, how it responds to our current needs. I believe the media of urban architecture and space cut through the booster hype with which we are inundated and get to the core of the urban condition.

Looking and listening closely to what the city says I am taken aback at how passively we submit to what is obviously an unacceptable condition. The cities I have seen are, despite extensive promotional literature to the contrary, engulfed in visual and aural confusion.

We wax eloquent when our wilderness is encroached upon, even if sometimes we lose the fight. For us, the natural environment is sacrosanct in literature and in our values. But when it come to the urban environment we are demonstratively mute. I do not ignore the infrequent efforts of professional planners and architects to describe the situation. Their efforts, nevertheless, remain genteel and behind the doors of their various conventions, little heeded by the public.

How conveniently we forget that the destruction of the wilderness is an indirect result of our urban habits. We merrily drive our vehicles, show off opulent condos while decrying the encroachment on the forests, sea shores and mountains.

Sincere environmentalist would never dream of abandoning their cars. Yet our profligate urban habits are the reason for much of the natural destruction.

It seems our cities are not places in which to ponder, but rather places to rush through and to get away from. Oh, we protest against every development. There is little difficulty arousing passionate objections to increased densities and high-rise development. It is not uncommon for people to be against high densities and at the same time fervently in favour of low-cost housing. Yet higher densities or housing people can afford in the downtown is the crux of the whole debate. Higher densities, mitigated by beautiful public urban space close to work may be one way of avoiding traffic congestion and high housing costs. Some of us dream of the city as an open greenspace park with us on the outside periphery looking in. Few bother to discern the contradiction.

The topic is of course complex and intricate. Many disciplines are involved — economics, social planning and more. An environmental breakdown may force us to change our habits; so much can happen that is beyond our control. As we continue to revere blindly technology and bureaucratic control, human error persists; witness the cities that are being buried in their own solid waste. Far more is involved than just the ambience of public urban space. Still, it is a very important starting place for us to learn to work together.

I contend the media of the city speak with a strong voice, because they tells us so much about ourselves. And that voice is saying chaos. How can we develop affordable, livable homes in the downtown in such an unfavourable environment? I hope that the statements made in this book will open a dialogue more relevant than the easy way out for the politicians and planners: palliatives, planting a few trees, laying down a bit of paving and painting up the store fronts.

The well-being of public urban space is crucial to the modern city if it is to become a place to live and work, a place to live in harmony and a place to work productively. The beauty and tranquillity of public urban spaces deserves the keenest consideration from our citizens, architects, planners and public administrators.

Roger Kemble.
Vancouver, B. C.

Acknowledgements

Many people provided the support, help and sustenance necessary to bring this book to the public. I was not as co-operative at times as I should have been. I would like to extend my warmest thanks and gratitude to the following people and institutions for the help they have afforded me. Although each contributed uniquely none are responsible for the views expressed here, which are my own. Joseph Baker, David Farley, Leonard Gertler, Maynard Gertler, Amy Kemble and Amanda Sarah Kemble gave their time, perceptive comments and guidance in reading the manuscript. Brahm Wiesman, although he was not directly involved, gave more than he would believe in bringing *The Canadian City* to fruition.

I am indebted to the Canada Council for their financial support of the initial research, to Canada Mortgage and Housing Corporation for the use of the table in appendix II, to Globe Press of Toronto for the data in appendix IV and to the City of Ottawa for the use of the chart in appendix III.

The following publishers and authors have graciously given permission to use quotations; Robert Allsopp, "On trying to make a silk purse out of a sow's ear. Trinity Park," *Landscape Architectural Review,* (December 1987); Margaret Atwood, "The City Planners," *The Circle Game,* (Toronto: Anansi, 1966); Joseph Baker, "There's more sizzle than substance in Safdie's musings," *The Gazette,* Montreal, (February 28, 1987); T. S. Eliot, "The Hollow Men, A penny for the old guy," *Selected Poems;* (London: Faber and Faber, 1954); and Elizabeth Godley, "Sculptures Vandalized," *The Vancouver Sun,* (June 10, 1988).

PART I
Art is Dead

1

A Personal View

Art is dead, at least the art of city design is dead!
    Our cities are chaotic. Doesn't everybody know? Our senses, where we live and work, are under constant bombardment. We survive a squalor of apparent affluence. We sustain the strain, we are inured to the consequences. Cacophony, noise and fractionate scenes are exploding. The city deteriorates before our eyes. Despite that, how do we respond? "Let's have a party", we say, "who the hell cares"! Then we regale the streets and boulevards with consumer emporiums, plastic malls and junk food eateries. How many boutiques, balloons, buntings, boats and biplanes can a healthy city stand?
    We expend millions on planning. We engage in public discussion ad nauseam. To what avail?
    No one wishes to be the purveyor of gloom, yet reluctant to acknowledge the cacophony we soldier stoically on. The Pollyanna attitude is destructive. Delusion is little comfort. We are safe from violence, our cities are peaceful. We gloat, gleefully comparing ourselves to blatant mayhem in the urban United States (appendix I, Noise Levels). We assuage our guilt by making comparisons to extreme conditions. We are so gentle; they are so violent. Yet, how can we be so self-satisfied? Is the quality of our cities to be measured by a lack of mayhem and by bodily safety?
    Self-satisfaction and delusion go beyond safety. We claim our cites are free from heavy urban debt loads. Yet, we fail to include the debt held by senior governments for essential work, or for bribing us with glittering projects that bring them short-lived kudos with no lasting return.
    The city in history has been a meeting place where peo-

ple gathered to create wealth. Now it is a cockpit where we wrestle with debt. No longer are our buildings proud evidence of the fruits of hard labour. They are symbols of devious tricks, usury and misplaced priorities. Our cities are victims of foolish financial policies, with under-utilized office buildings, twenty percent vacant: regional highs, thirty-five per cent. Vacant building sites and parking lots are used as poker chips in a speculative game defying economic sense. Sidewalks, sewers and roads deteriorate because they lack charisma to be an issue. Decaying stocks of inexpensive housing, people living aimless street lives are in contrast to trendy condos. This is a culture going broke.

4 Are there obscure, international financial formulae that escape my understanding? Perhaps these esoteric lacunae assure the silent investor all is well. Perhaps all is well. What, then, accounts for the obviously deteriorating urban and cultural environment? What about our peace of mind? Is the visual chaos, is the aural chaos, appendix I, to be shrugged off? What about the unavoidable dilapidation of our parks, our older buildings, the things that make the city comfortably our own? What about the sheer ugliness? Can we escape by partying forever?

We should take a closer look. The city, its buildings and things is a medium of communication. The whole conglomeration informs us of our cultural and economic well-being. Our cities reflect our living and working lore; they describe the manner in which we live. Architecture of the cities: the buildings, roads, parks, spaces, alleys, lamp posts, hydrants, all the touchable, visible fixed things, are headlines like the newspaper or the television media, except there is a subtle difference. The architecture of the city, the way it is interrelated, the way we weave its weft and warp cannot be edited to suit some purpose. When the city cries, what it says it means; no double speak there.

Today, the architecture of contemporary Canadian cities is in crisis. Cities have become repositories of mindless imported whims. Whims promoted as profitable, international, architectural sophistication. Nothing could be farther from the truth.

Canadian cities do not sustain the appellations "world class", "international", or other flack invented phrases. Buildings and the cities are weak symbols of overpowering, destructive, out-of-control, artless international finance gone

berserk. Current buildings respond with manic immediacy to
ephemeral fads, sticking to the city like lint on a worn out suit.
Dubbed "sophisticated international style", architecture has
degenerated into aimless, formless mass-produced, all-too-
tangible apparitions, rooted in write-offs and tax dodges, the
product of harassed minds clinging tenuously to imagined reality. Masquerading as authentic, the architecture of the modern city is *apatride* with no loyalties, no ideals, no responsibility
to those who use it or to those who need more than it can
offer. Our cites are encumbered by these useless hulks. They
are the architecture of illusion, the mirage of private gain,
accumulating the reality of public debt. The cities and the
hulks they host are symbolic of cultural demoralization. They
ominously represent our current architectural tastes, *haute-
vulgarité*.

5

This mirage is in the suburbs too. In the countryside,
wherever we go, nothing is sacred. Our most dearly held values are manicured, mortgaged lawns, cardboard fronts, mir-
roring sound sets for the soaps, gluttonous auto ways raked
by motorized pesky metal midgets, eating up land and ubiquitous going-out-of-business, hanging on by the skin of their
teeth, plastic malls.

The mirage is self perpetuating. Responding to the inse-
curity-revealing ever-asked question "How do you like your
city"? the city dweller usually says something nice, uncon-
sciously innocuous. No one wants to bad mouth home. Like
my friend from the big city. He loves the big city, that is very
evident. His answer is suitably evasive—"Because there are so
many escape routes to the cottage". His answer is a coded
message that says, "Well now this is my home; I've lived here
all my life; I have invested the place with trust and emotions;
my family and friends make me feel needed; I am not lonely.
But . . ." and then comes the good stuff. West Coasters answer with "skiing, sailing, swimming close to home". How
often do they say they love the streets, the buildings, or the
little interesting spaces they have discovered for themselves.
Oh yes, they like that little restaurant "round the corner".
But invariably the city proper is a void in our imaginations.
We have subliminally blanked it out.

There are muted cries of warning. Not everyone is myopic. Not all are at the party. Some gentle souls raise a voice in
protest. The Prince of Wales is one. Recently, in no uncertain
terms, he told the collected architects and planners of Brit-

ain what he thought. "Can't you see what you are doing"? he remonstrated. To which they replied pompously, "The Prince is ill-informed". Baloney! It is they who are ill-informed.

Earlier, he had dubbed the proposed addition to the National Gallery "a carbuncle on the face of Trafalgar Square", and if it goes ahead it will be.

We need not seek abroad for sensitive understanding. In Montreal, Joseph Baker, an architect and advocate, described his own city in *The Gazette* as "our own ravaged, ruptured, scandalously mistreated, once so fine city".

Ah Montreal. "When I think about those nights in Montreal". Well, Gino perhaps you'd better go home and take a look in day-time. You'll sing a different tune. Someone is dismantling the place.

6

The once so fine Montreal is a several-layered city, now lying there almost in ruins. Each layer is imposed on top of the other. Fractionated separation is the style. The old city, the earliest layer surrounding place d'Armes, is separated from the new and newest cities. Dominion Square with its broken denture skyline is the new layer and place Ville Marie represents the newest layer.

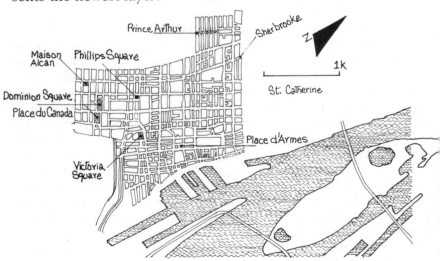

Figure 1.   Montreal Québec

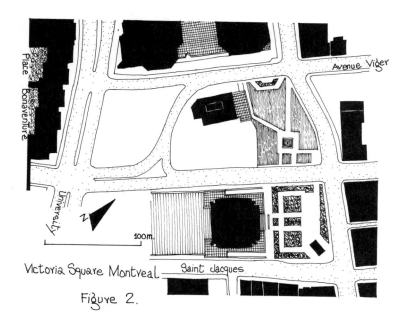

Victoria Square Montreal

Figure 2.

Urban separation in Montreal is also topographical. The land the city occupies is contoured, rising up from the river, in terraces. The old city occupies *la terrasse inférieure,* on the river. The new and newer cities occupy *la terrasse supérieure,* around Mount Royal. Chronologically, the new city is represented by the buildings of the twenties and thirties. Figure **1,** Montreal, Québec, gives a generalized view of those few downtown blocks that are known to the bureaucrats as *centre-ville.*

The separations are distinct. What could once have been a beautiful link bridging the separation is confusing in the spatial effect of Victoria Square. This amorphous expanse of undefined cacophonous space was once an hay market. Right now it looks like nowhere.

The square, **2,** is shown in plan as if we were in a helicopter looking down from above. The black shapes are the footprint plans of the buildings. The hatched shapes are grassy area gardens. Dots represent paved roads. The surrounding buildings are shown in **3,** looking towards the north and **4,** looking south. The high-rise in **3,** is the 180-metre tower la Tour de la Bourse.

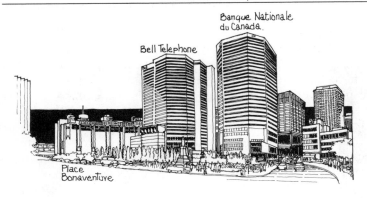

Bell Telephone

Banque Nationale
du Canada.

Place
Bonaventure

Figure 3.   Victoria Square, Montreal,
Looking North.

Walking through Victoria Square inspires the pedestrian to lament a sense of leftover space. No one can think what to do, so plant a bit of grass to keep the locals quiet. The effect is of an abandoned city lot. Yet it is an important space. No doubt, developers consider it to be a prestigious address. Transportation lines converge there. The old city is linked to the new city at this place. It is an important space in an important city with the ambience of a neglected ruin.

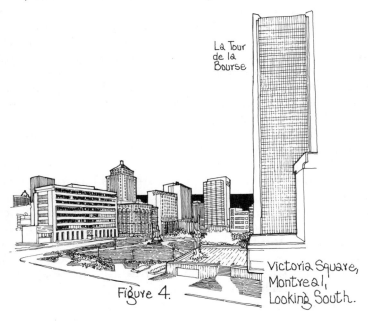

La Tour
de la
Bourse

Figure 4.   Victoria Square,
Montreal,
Looking South.

Still, people who use the space are resilient. They make do with what is there. They walk, rest, eat lunch in summertime. In that general area they have nowhere else to go. The place is a desolate chunk of snow in winter. Surrounded by traffic noise and discordant buildings, it is a place to leave behind quickly.

To repair Victoria Square planners will have to contend with unrelated, domineering buildings, la Tour, la Banque Nationale and Bell. They will have to contend with freeways underneath and the ventilation shafts. Excessive noise and traffic confusion must be mitigated. Those old chopped-up buildings must be replaced by something useful; restore the ones worth saving and make the new ones useful. They will have to contend with the radical change in scale, melding the face of the old city with the back side of the new.

In this respect Victoria Square is a microcosm of its city. Planning its renewal presents quite a challenge! According to Montreal architect Melvin Charney, there are 250 named public urban spaces in the city. Some you wouldn't recognize as such; others, mostly in the old city, have an incomparable ambient beauty. If Victoria Square presents a planning challenge, what of all the others?

The city has not been careful in caring for them. Most of the city's spaces are in a state of separated animation, as though half-constructed and neglected for lack of interest. Each era, each building within that era seems to have been a separate act in defiance of the city. The new city of the last two decades, comprised of undistinguished vulgar corporate hulks, is imposed upon a mass of sulking desolate buildings, built after the grand dominating national finance era of the old city. Open spaces have been treated in the same way. Victoria Square is a demonstration of the rampant disregard. The whole manifests sensory overkill.

The urban state of Montreal can be interpreted as a microcosm of the urban state of the country? The chaos of Montreal presages the condition of cities. If we pay careful attention to the media of urban Montreal we can hear the muted protestations of all our cities. It speaks of an ostensibly cultural, economically healthy people feigning reality. 'Architecture', Ruskin said, 'is the mother of all art'. What then is the condition of the other arts if the architecture is in such a state?

Other arts and other cities are, indeed, no better. Throughout the country the ambience is hectic, running

9

roughshod over our sensibilities. The excitement is craven. Troglodytic city workers have overdosed on consumer opulence. We are goggle-eyed, pit-lamped by trendy things. What we can't afford we plasticize. A never-ending string of galas, stadia, places for the people, glut our sensibilities, always for "the people". Anything to satisfy an indulged body politic. Manic we sit glazed at any spectacle put before us.

Large projects are proposed for every vacant piece of city land. Inner city rail-yards and industrial tracts are obsolete. Massive proposals are planned to replace them. Only time will tell how great these projects will be. For now they do not look good. There have been too many false starts and abandonments to be complacent. The Regina rail-yards have been abandoned. Whatever happened to the bassin Louise housing project? On the Expo lands in Vancouver they have tried three or four times and only now have they started to do something. The Toronto Harbourfront development has been the subject of an enquiry; what went wrong?

10

Figure 5. Harbourfront Toronto

The Toronto Harbourfront lands, **5,** are what remains of obsolescent, waterfront industrial rail-yards. The illustration is a birds-eye view of the development from above the lake. The CN Tower is in the middle. Queen's Quay Terminal is on the right and to the left of the CN Tower are the three controversial condominium towers. Behind them is the Skydome stadium. The development covers eighty-one hectares on the waterfront from Yonge to Bathurst.

Harbourfront's relation to downtown Toronto is shown in **6,** Toronto, Ontario. The overall idea of how the land has been built up to 1988 is depicted in **7,** Harbourfront & Railway Lands, Toronto, Ontario. The black areas represent completed building footprints and the wavy area is Lake Ontario.

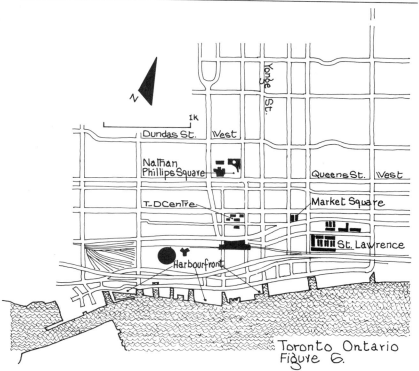

Toronto Ontario
Figure 6.

    That parcel of land has been difficult to plan from the start. A lineal strip of land squeezed between the Gardiner Expressway, the intercontinental railway, and the waterfront,

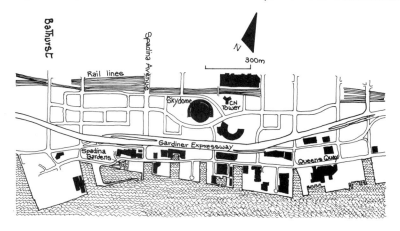

Figure 7. Harbourfront & Railway Lands Toronto Ont.

with docks intruding to break up the spaces. Yet the badly conceived plan layout cannot be attributed to the site, difficult as it may be, because none of the existing site characteristics have been used to advantage. Indeed the site has been ignored in favour of a development conception that could be anywhere. Clusters could have been arranged in spatial groups around the pier indentations, but this is not the case. Instead the road cuts the piers off at their most disadvantaged location. The layout is just another exercise in conventional planning, no spirit, no imagination. (Does this tell us about the real state of the city lurking under the glitter?).

_12_   Queen's Quay West would have been better located under the Gardiner Expressway, combined with Lake Shore Boulevard, with feeder roads branching off to service buildings on the waterfront. The relentless lineality of the development would then have been alleviated, to say nothing of the traffic pollution. Opportunities for well-proportioned urban clusters would have materialized around each quay. The ensuing clustered buildings would have tempered the effects of the large, inevitable, high-rise buildings and managed the use of urban spaces.

Harbourfront is a new use for that old part of the city. Using the existing road layout as it is has been a mistake. Traffic, transportation and the traffic engineer have first priority, as always. . . . Think of living first, leave the traffic for later—for the roads have taken up the most desirable sites. Harbourfront, like the rest of the city, is built for the traffic not for people, flourishing publicity notwithstanding.

Harbourfront buildings are sprinkled haphazardly within a _mélange_ of meagre, architecturally inconsequential, structures. Despite their size, the high-rise towers emit a meagre lack of spirit.

Apprehensions have traditionally run high against the high-rise buildings yet their form has validity if not in the way it is handled here. The high rises are not what is wrong for there is no well thought out plan for living. There are no spaces, no plazas, no places that become naturally recognizable. The western end of Harbourfront is surrounded by amorphous shapes, isolated by rampaging traffic and raked by shrapnel-crackling winds off the lake. What space there is, other than the leftover fun-palace waste land is a quaint little park, Spadina Gardens.

Spadina Gardens is a valiant effort by the designers to overcome hopeless odds. They never had a chance. Fighting noisy traffic, hemmed in by a hectic speedway, exposed to the raking elements, overlooked by innocuous buildings, the designers did the best they could. And their penchant to use lukewarm architectural idioms (gratuitously borrowed from the international glossies) divested the work of any originality. Spadina reflects our specious times.

Harbourfront shows how we abhor sensitive considered planning, how impressed we are by the "get rich quick snake-oil salesmen". It also shows the drawbacks of our misplaced approbation. Oh how much we revere the shallow thinker. Reposed and peaceful planning is ideological anathema. And then we ask what happened? But there it is. A civic predicament calling for an enquiry.

13

What went wrong is endemic, at the heart of those popular urban delusions. More than a congenial group of well-meaning citizens will be needed to find the answer. We can hope the enquiry will delve beneath the surface and that it will not dissipate constructive dissent. Some good may come of it yet.

Other cities deserve abrasive scrutiny too. Torontonians are brave to address their misgivings openly. They send a message to us all; when there is enough civic confusion it cannot be ignored. We are too complacent and smug to be absolved. Western cities are no better. An entrenched small-town smugness prevails. Winnipeg, Calgary, Vancouver and the rest, are all in civic disarray. Yet to hear them crow you'd think the angels were on their very doorstep.

In Vancouver, Pacific Place like Harbourfront is about to become a huge developed urban agglomeration. The portents are ominous. The current designs reflect more a layout for a suburban shopping mall than a living addition to the downtown of a vibrant growing city. Streets wind like little subdivision backwaters. One of them is bound to be named "Wyndy Wynde" sooner or later. Green spaces are dotted around liberally but they are undefined; no one really knows what to do with them. No one would believe they serve high-rise buildings far beyond the scale of the street. And the high-rise buildings, too, are sprinkled about, completely unrelated to one another, as though they surround a low meandering, amorphous shopping mall with the inevitable parking rink like those that litter the suburbs.

We are so used to building in the suburbs we have forgotten the city. There is no public awareness or demand for well-designed public urban spaces, consequently the developers can get away with any old plan. And competence in planning is measured by getting planning approval, not by creating a well-designed series of urban spaces. No one knows any better.

14

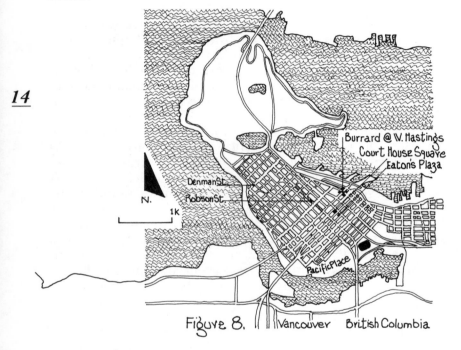

Figure 8. Vancouver British Columbia

Pacific Place in relationship to downtown Vancouver is shown on figure **8**. Until the early 1970s the land upon which it is to be built was railway land. The completed project will cover eighty-two hectares on the north shore of False Creek, the erstwhile venue of Expo 86. A more detailed plan of the area, all ninety-one hectares, the Stadium, Expo Legacy Buildings and the Round House is illustrated in figure **9**.

Since the CPR announced removal of the rail-yards nearly twenty years ago there have been five full-blown development proposals (including Expo 86) for that site. The current embryonic plans and models (exhibited in the spring of 1988) look okay. Reposeful residential space is evident, protected from distressful noisy roadways. The potential is there. For

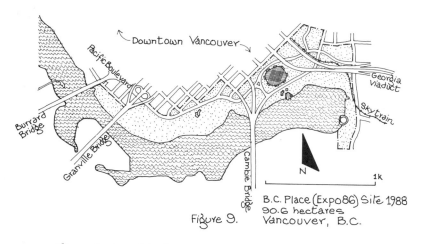

Figure 9.   B.C. Place (Expo86) Site 1988
90.6 hectares
Vancouver, B.C.

15

once, the relationship between work life and living is recognized. Residential enclaves contained by the winding road make spaces for harmonious living but they show the potential for becoming expensive ghettos. North Park, in the northeast corner, **10,** now just a mass of blacktop, will transform into what is euphemistically dubbed International Village.

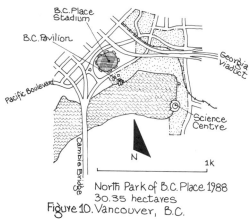

Figure 10.   North Park of B.C. Place 1988
30.35 hectares
Vancouver, B.C.

No doubt about it, lessons have been learned in the long drawn out process since the CPR's announcement. But there is still a long way to go. The mature civic memory will still detect the perfidious art of sophistry. We have been this road before. Who knows what disruptions will occur in the upcoming decades. T. S. Eliot knew:

Between the conception
And the creation
Between the emotion
And the response
Falls the shadow.

How will they sell the high-priced condos, the expensive offices in chaotic circumstances? Nothing in the glitzy presentation addresses the causes of current urban blight. Pretty model to the contrary, overbearing traffic and disjointed spaces are still potentially there. The stadium will not be a peaceful neighbour; the blown-up roof transmits noise across the city. Rock concerts can be heard, free of charge, from miles away.

The plan demonstrated no understanding of how public urban space can be integrated with the street pattern as an amenity that adds to the pleasure of living in the city. The architectural renderer, the architectural model maker has usurped the process once again. We must be wary. Attractive as the presentations may be, there is reason to be apprehensive.

The existing road layout is already overbearing. Sharing fault with Harbourfront, the Pacific Place traffic engineers took over where the realtors should have been. If we ever learn we learn the hard way. Before development starts, choice land is already encased in blacktop. The Georgia Viaduct, the Cambie Bridge and the Granville Bridge cut into the choice parts of the site. Pacific Boulevard has already dissected the best living places with traffic noise and smell.

Making traffic the only priority has changed the city. We are prisoners to the chimerical freedom of auto travel. The root cause of our abrasive urban environment is our unwillingness to treat traffic in relation to other important priorities. Nothing exhibited in the transportation fair at Expo 86 demonstrated a willingness to address the chaotic influence of traffic on the city. The fair was a pathetic lost opportunity amidst trivial promotion on that count. The organizers' preoccupation for numbers at the expense of any content at all exposed the profound contempt those organizers had for the people who ultimately paid for the fair.

Expo 86 was a party. We were supposed to have fun and learn something in the bargain. Transportation was supposed to be the theme. The turnstiles whirled with happy-go-lucky consumers, lurching for soft seats and anonymity. Superannuated, skateboarding scallywags, saucer-eyed pretty girls— we were dazzled by the flashing lights and the big screens. We revealed how easily we could be distracted by glittering TV shadows. Not a word about the city and its transportation. No legacy left on the site to prepare us for a well-developed downtown place.

Everything was on time, on budget. The numbers crunched. The flack had all the fun; they soared above the roof tops. Hi-tech innovation, they said, on the leading edge of the Pacific, the world. How sad!

We learned little about ourselves too. We ate a lot. We watched. Pavilions, heaped in random, set up what were supposed to be streets that meandered and were paved with spilt *17* slurpees. Roof pipes, bent like straws, littered the skyline, balloons wafted in the breeze. The whole thing took on the appearance of a windblown forest of flimsy pipes, dumped on by an erinaceous goofball. Not much to demonstrate the future of the city. Not much future city transportation.

The centrepiece of Expo 86 was a metaphor of the whole: Canada Place, the waterborne convention centre and cruise ship facility. Imagine it to be a sailing ship; some do. It has inadvertently rammed the dock under full sail. As a confused wreck of architectural, disjointed forms its downed rigging festoons the deck; its bow erupts upward. Popular trend setters would have us believe that this is urban beauty yet the subliminal media message is anything but.

Expo 86 was indicative of the urban hysteria of the eighties: shallow, graceless and temporary, a demonstration of the triumph of ignorance. Highway 86, that inimical symbol, expressed it with profundity: a flat concrete surface emerged from the murky waters of False Creek. Undulating, grey, littered with the discarded techno-detritus of industrial society, it ended up between two freeways. Ignominiously it languished, prodding up between them, frayed concrete and re-bars, going absolutely nowhere. The artist always gets the last laugh and the fair organizers are tragically unaware the joke is on them.

Pacific Place is to be built on the site left over from Expo 86. Hopefully, new ideas will miraculously materialize to shake Vancouver from its smug complacency. Where is Joachim Foikis when we need him!

The modern city of the eighties is emerging as a mass of

separated buildings, for whatever reason. Neither at Expo, nor at Harbourfront was an attempt made to demonstrate the wholeness of the city; just the same decades-old stuff, the same mistakes. Buildings become separated from one another. Each building design striving to outdo the other, but always banal, always ordinary. Urban space is left-over space.

Urban spaces that are fractionated are those spaces that have become so disorganized, so badly designed we have difficulty recognizing them as urban places at all. Modern cities abound with them. Parks, squares, plazas, lanes, the streets have become disjointed, disrupted by traffic, surrounded by ugly buildings, so filled with noise, so brash they can hardly be called places any more. We rush away from them. Buildings on the streets bear no relation to their neighbours. We see the city as a collection of things that fill holes in empty spaces, or tubes to get from here to there.

A contemporary individualistic penchant for seeing things in broken pieces, for breaking the city up into arbitrary specialized pieces, is one reason why urban space is ignored. The separateness of our thinking embedded in the design of buildings, despite arguable economic pressures, militates against an improved living environment. A somnambulating penchant for judging buildings and urban space from photographs instead of from reality may also be a contributing factor. Understanding public urban spaces and a sense of urban place, breaking out of the separated thinking syndrome, is the key to seeing the whole.

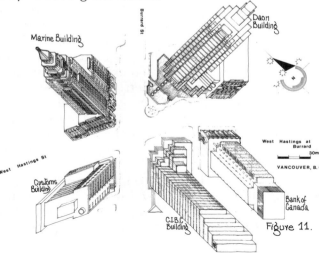

Figure 11.

Yet hard as they are to find there are some fine urban streets. West Hastings in Vancouver is one. There are some fine buildings on that street. Yet separateness, brought on by modernity, at the intersection, **11,** was inevitable.

Developed in the 1920s, West Hastings ultimately succumbed to a break-down of space, although between Granville and Hornby the beauty of the traditional alignment is preserved. But to the west, and around the corner on Burrard, modern blandness exerts its ugly image. The intersection shows what has happened and what could have been. The Marine Building flows around its corner gently. The four modern buildings in staccato lurches lunge around their corners and show how separateness has become the norm. The modern buildings do nothing for the street. They stand alone in chaotic isolation.

19

The Marine Building, on the north-west corner is a beautiful late 1920s art deco design built by McCarter and Nairn, Architects. The facade is designed to be attractive to the pedestrian at the street. Above eye level the building blossoms into a tiered tower. The street facade turns the corner and the whole building turns with it. The tower is crowned by a patinated copper roof. Now that is urban architecture.

The intersection at Portage and Main in Winnipeg, **12,** is succumbing to the same quasi-economic influences as those

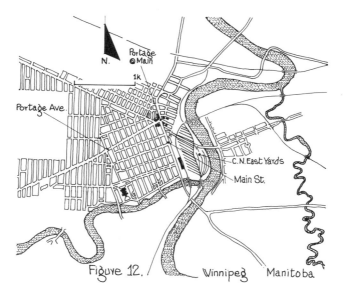

Figure 12. / Winnipeg Manitoba

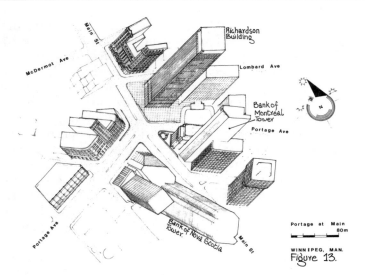

Portage at Main
80m

WINNIPEG, MAN.
Figure 13.

at Hastings and Burrard. Whatever a sense of place may have been, Winnipeg has lost it. The old streets have disappeared. The city is one big parking lot now. Portage and Main, **13,** reflects the ensuing fractured spaces. Tall concrete and glass towers deny their neighbours' presence. Each cries for individual attention. Ungraceful concrete barricades separate pedestrian from vehicles. The intersection is infested with horrendously busy traffic. There is no vantage point from which to see the buildings. No one in their right mind would linger on that noisy, busy, hard, cold corner. Only the new Bank of Montreal Tower and its old porticoed banking hall is designed with a modicum of sensitivity.

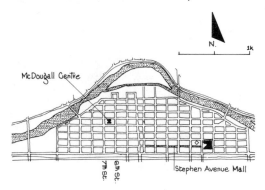

Figure 14. Calgary Alberta.

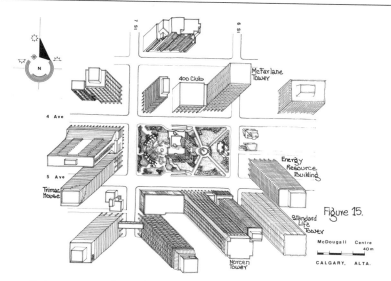

Figure 15.

McDougall Centre
40m

CALGARY, ALTA.

Other examples of broken isolation can be found without much effort. Calgary is a separated city, by virtue of its very rigid layout, **14.** Yet McDougall Centre, **15,** survives as one of a very few urban spaces left. No harassing traffic in the Mac-Dougall garden. Still, separate buildings inevitably surround it standing sentinel to coldness and isolation.

The sense of separateness persists. In this at least the Canadian city can be said to be "in the world class". Architec-

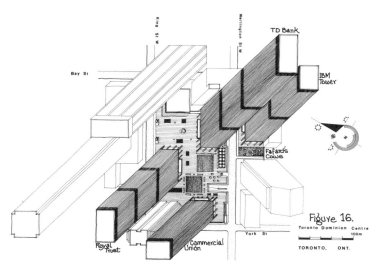

Figure 16.

Toronto Dominion Centre
100m

TORONTO, ONT.

tural national symbols show off our subliminal carelessness. What can be said of the urban spaces created by the presence of the National Arts Centre, Roy Thompson Hall, the Toronto Dominion Centre or Westmount Square, except to say they are bereft of any.

The TD Centre, **16,** can be said to be both magnificent and majestic. Located on the corner of King Street West and Bay Street (conceived in 1967), it was expected to become a symbol for future development in Toronto. The towers are awe inspiring; they are pristine. To say the least, the centre promotes itself as a place of great financial deliberations and a repository of a distinctive art collection. And because it is all of these the TD complex cannot be ignored as architecture, urban space or art.

Architect Mies van der Rohe was chosen for his international reputation to design the complex. But choice of architect notwithstanding, all the wrongs embodied in contemporary urban art and space are exemplified in this pristine complex of buildings. It may seem perverse to describe this complex as magnificent and majestic then use it to disrobe the shortcomings of contemporary art. But indeed it is the perfect media example of the cold separated aloofness that typifies the structure of our urban lives. Margaret Atwood knows why:

> ... what offends us is
> the sanities:
> the houses in pedantic rows, the planted
> sanitary trees, assert
> levelness of surface like a rebuke. ...

The spatial ambience is pristine and monstrous. The highest tower is 229 metres. The complex is just over one-and-a-half hectares of plaza. The proportions have been worked out to the letter. Even for Toronto the scale is massive, yet it is appropriate for its use and is in keeping with the area. Height alone does not make it monstrous, nor does the size of the plaza. The monstrous ambience comes from combining unrecognizable, vertical, monotone, oppressive architectural forms. Interaction, the essence of urban space and art, is suppressed, muted and bland. Indeed there is none.

Promotional literature announced the centre as "almost a touchstone of Canadian national identity and Toronto's civic pride". Why that is so is not explained. Such architecture

22

is obscure; indeed it is the very *apatride* rootless architecture that impairs urban beauty throughout the world. National identity is difficult to recognize in a building that is essentially no different from van der Rohe's ascetic statements in New York or Chicago and his attempt to burden the City of London with an identical tower.

"Toronto's civic pride" is to some degree understandable for, have little doubt, this is an imposing achievement of sorts. It is not an effete private icon of cherished corporate success. Or perhaps it is! And if that is so then corporate urban responsibility should be taken more seriously. Lack of insight cannot be rationalized in promotional literature.

Pristine magnificence is the corollary of chaos. Mies was a master at obfuscating both. He had the ability to seduce his public with pleasant one-liners, "Milk can be cold but not architecture". He made life easy for himself by reducing his architectural program and ignoring real life conditions. With fastidious coldness he was able to transform the warmth of the human spirit into hard steel. We went along unwittingly. The remorselessly vertical application of the steel I sections to every surface is the outcome of his penchant for thinking in aphorisms.

23

The monotone shadows of the TD Centre defy human emotional response. Colour in the marble of the plaza and in the art and planting is too weak to counteract the overwhelming cavity of darkness. The blackness absorbs light and our human emotions. The cavity of blackness evokes an emotion of pervasive exploitation, a feeling of human inadequacy. We are so small. The vertical decoration accentuates our smallness. We are vulnerable on the plaza as the wind slices into us. This sunless plaza in the city is better appreciated in the subterranean mall below, for the ambient feeling on the plaza is don't touch, do your work and go away.

This is not a peaceful plaza despite the static architectural composition. Noise pervades the entire space. Taken at the quietest time, noise level readings are too high (appendix I). Weekday noise levels are even higher. Peripheral passing traffic noise resonating off the hard smooth surfaces amplifies the levels into a range of seventy-eight decibels. Sound tends to reverberate from surface to surface. In a residential environment noises of the level on the TD plaza would be debilitating. Probably they are debilitating in this work environment too. We have yet to understand the implications of urban noise. Have we, in self defence, inured our sensibilities? We work, and sometimes live, in a hectic environment. Can art make it softer on our lives? Are corporate art collections able to humanize the buildings? Do the collectibles gracing the TD Centre mitigate the noise, scale, imposing space and monotone colour?

The TD Bank displays public art on the plazas and in the public lobbies. The art displayed is a benign collection of decorator's choice carriage trade craft. Controversy has been avoided. Controversy is not a requisite of art. Communication is. And this display communicates the bland repressed compliance that is its hallmark.

24 Current public art in Canada is clearly lucrative for the participating artists. Doing art is reason enough to be an "artist". But the point of art is not in the doing but rather in the burning passion of having something to say, something to contribute. The art of the TD Centre, the architecture of the centre itself, says nothing beyond current platitudes. What is the point of art if it fails to challenge the intellect of the beholder? Why not just stick posters on the walls.

The art does nothing for the spaces. Nothing can humanize the buildings, neither does it mitigate the imposing magniloquence. It languishes inconsequentially on the surfaces, shrouded by the black, vertical ennui of the space. There simply isn't enough of it to share the immensity of the centre. Art is what should amplify our human instincts but at the TD Centre it is treated as gratuitous froth implanted to dispel rumblings of dissatisfaction.

The arcane, geometric structure, on the King Street plaza is probably a homage to credit henge. On the side of the IBM tower, stuck between the buildings, are Joe Fafard's lamenting cows. Haphazardly placed on the lobby walls are some wall hangings, variously coloured—foiling, no doubt, the morose magniloquence of the architecture.

Fafard's cows, seven of them, **16,** diminished and huddled, are stuffed away, irrelevantly, on a sunless, dank plot overpowered by banal buildings on Wellington Street. Have these cows been placed to give reason to an awkward space or do they make a contribution? Is their contribution to fill an overlooked chunk of expensive downtown real estate? Perhaps, for the cows look surprised, as if to say, "What the hell are we doing here"? Like the ingenue who came home from the Olympics with a gold and had it bronzed, the cows, like the gold, are bronzed and they deserve better treatment. Their over-scaled multiple forms could be put to better purpose. The cows could be a grand and humorous antidote to the imposing ambience of the complex if they were sited on the main plaza grass, highlighted by occasional sunshine. What an effect they would have on the latent arrogance of the plaza! Like the horses of Saint Marks they could find a place in history as the cows of Saint Bank. They deserve the comparison. Ominously, legend has it, reclining cows portend bad weather. Do the bankers know that?

We must accept that art and architecture are inseparable in more than book form. Architecture is the living environment. Art is the communicator of our prowess. Public art and public space are inseparable.

25

Public art, for so long, has been relegated to remembrance of the dead. The closest many of us can come to public art is the war memorial. In every city in the maritimes dying soldiers and roaring cannons regale each space and corner. Halifax reminds us Mafeking has been relieved, and thank God, for it is so easy to forget. In Montreal's Victoria Square, Queen Victoria effects her benign Thatcheresque pose. Kings, Queens and war dead have become our treasures. They are our civic art. We appreciate them as beautiful sculptured artifacts. That's about all we have left.

Indeed recent public art has become arcane and indecipherable. The current obscurantism in the name of public art helps to accentuate the fragmented separateness of urban spaces. Artists build their pieces to celebrate "the people", so they say. They always do it for people. More often than not the public is left dumbfounded. Terry Johnson, director at Emily Carr College of Art, was quoted in *The Vancouver Sun* telling of his students' opinion, "I don't tend to hear a lot of grousing about the quality of public art [in Vancouver]. The students tend to ignore it". They should know.

Art, whether it is private or public, is a matter of risk. Artists stick their necks out to make a point. Art must have something to say, something to impart as a challenge to the viewer, if only to mitigate the contemporary urban malaise. If you don't believe me catch Tadashi Kawamata's temporary fling at the Colonial Tavern cavity on Yonge Street in Toronto.

Contemporary art has regressed into esoteric abstractions that have relieved the artist of his responsibility to risk and to commit. The choice of public art in buildings has become a matter for the decorator. Current public art is void of content. The artist hides behind sophistry and intellectual posturing. The artist's message has become so weak as to defy attention. Contemporary public art has degenerated into distraction. National culture is nothing if our public buildings are so oppressive the only function left for art is to foil contemporary architectural monstrosities.

Victoria Square, the TD Centre, Portage and Main, McDougall Centre, and West Hastings and Burrard demonstrate one root cause of the chaos in the city. The buildings stand alone, the architecture of separateness. Applied public art does not alleviate the sense of separateness. We must rethink the city. Better we design our urban spaces so buildings and public art share space. We must cultivate a shared vision of urban space for the future.

26

2

A Shared Vision of Urban Space

A shared vision of urban space is a cultural consensus acknowledged in the urban community. It is a lingering respect
for the work of our fathers. It guides the way as a series of
signposts to a future of non-intrusive and useful developments. When a community enjoys balanced social, political
and economic concerns, energy is released bringing into
reach finer aspects of urban life. That release allows us to enjoy the economic benefits of a well ordered urban life creating
new places for us to work and live and to preserve and keep
useful those that were built before.

Well, that is pretty fancy. How do we get there? Clearly
what was once taken for granted in the urban development
process is being ignored. Take for instance any of the beautiful public urban spaces built previous to our own era.

These very beautiful urban spaces accumulated over centuries sometimes. Each builder had an unstated subliminal
respect for other buildings. Yet they did not have to endure
the enervating delays of guide-lines, meetings and approvals.
Why? Because the community shared a vision for its urban
surroundings.

A shared vision of urban space is a statement of mission.
It is an agreement among a number of affected people as to
what they expect from a set of design guide-lines that affect
their area.

Some believe sharing a vision of urban space is as remote
to our current values as the Flying Dutchman was to a landfall.
A golden rule in Canadian politics states: "When two or more
Canadians gather to deliberate someone else's money gets
spent"—demonstrating there are pitfalls even when we try.

If by a miracle we all, tomorrow, decide to agree how our

urban spaces should be, our urban environment will improve, no doubt. But without an idea of what to share we will not be much farther ahead. More than talk is necessary. We must commit to sharing ideas and understand what that means. Developing such an understanding of values is a socio-cultural phenomenon, a wonder the social engineers must keep well away from. Such a spontaneous outbreak of public awareness is more than an easy-to-understand simple process. Questions arise out of the process more than answers. Who do we share with? How do we communicate to one another? Who will be included in the sharing? What if current tastes are formalized into that vision, *haute-vulgarité* and all that. What then? And God help us if they are.

28   At city hall large offices with many willing planners have worked for years to regulate development. We have invested our hopes and expectations in regulations to make our dreams come true. And we are disappointed. Regulations have merely institutionalized bad habits. How could regulations have improved the urban environment anyway? Nothing tangible is evident. They just illuminate the fact that we never had any dreams in the first place; expediency seemed so easy. All we have had are covetous expectations. Heaven knows badly designed cities are more virulent and prevalent than before the planners existed. Municipal planning processes notwithstanding, the negative conditions have magnified.

Planning procedures are ineffective because we lack direction. In response to our lack of vision, too many planners see their jobs as paper work. A collectively agreed upon understanding of urban space is simply not a part of their agenda and we just let things slide.

Firing planners and discarding regulations will not help. Sooner or later we must run out of scapegoats. In fairness, their job smooths out the process, putting our dreams into effect. They are, ultimately, responsible to us. We need planners; we need regulations. But they must have direction. We must rethink their purpose and direct them with a vision. If we don't share a vision and demonstrate it clearly no one will stick their necks out for us.

Most of us do have some vaguely formed idea of what we would like our city to be. Generally, we are more articulate at what we're against than what we're for. Few of us will concede the city of today is a beautiful environment. Most of us dream of escaping. What vision we sometimes harbour is rooted in heritage, something that never was, but is charming when fixed up. We go off in droves to Europe to admire the beautified remnants of baroque city boulevards, open spaces and squares. We judge other cultures in history on the vision they left behind for us to enjoy. What vision of space is left for us in our cities today is often the legacy of past eras. We live, carrion-like, off the past.

No urban vision is more appreciated than the remains of London and Paris. The remains developed during the reigns of the Georges and Napoleons. The Georgian Londoners had a vision of urban space. So did Napoleon's Parisians. True their civic debt loads were more exotic than our own. Their city was a few tidy mews and grand alleys; leave the main streets and their anarchy was worse than ours. The clatter of horses' hooves on cobble-stone streets, no doubt, rang cadenzas on the ear drums.

29

We cannot rely on a vision that probably never existed for our vision of the cities. The Georgian Londoners were motivated by the simple expedience of following upper class conformity. When the Regent wanted glory, hang the expense, he built his own Royal Mile. His vision of urban space, Regent Street, Portland Place and Regent's Park, figure **17,** bolted through old London from Carlton House to his newly-dreamed-up Regent's Park, regardless of expense, regardless of the less fortunate. The French had brought glory to Paris;

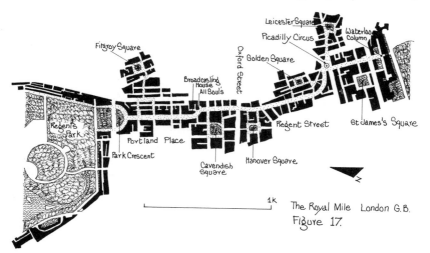

The Royal Mile London G.B.
Figure 17.

he wasn't about to be outdone. That is as good a motivation for sharing an idea of the city as we can expect to get, even today. But the Georges and Napoleons ignored so much and excluded so many; we cannot withstand such disparity. So our own shared vision must be imaginative, tailored for ourselves. It is not going to happen quickly.

Most of us enjoy the sharing of that vision after the fact. We borrow heavily. All the hard work was done in a bygone era. We leave the risks to others. Risk there was on Regent Street for its urban beauty did not come about without upheaval. There was no common consensus, the works just pushed through the old medieval city. Many habits were rearranged. And the conveniently, acquiescent, John Nash the architect, was ignominiously awarded the design not for his talent, such is the rumour, but for tolerating the Regent's philandering dalliance with his wife.

Regent Street and Portland Place, **17,** proceed from the Waterloo Column to Park Crescent. Regardless, they thrust into the labyrinth and warrens of the old town. The flanking new buildings on either side were massive in their times. The scale of the new street imposed on the medieval layout. The imbalance was abrupt, an intrusion of a differently scaled, strangely direct pattern. The traditional city was imposed upon suddenly, much in the same way we experience new skyscrapers imposed upon our cities now.

Scale then, however, did not consume the older areas as developments do today. And time has brought about a melding of the medieval city and the Regency. Since the intrusion there has been a healing process between the old mess of small streets and the sinuous thrust of the new. They emerged pervasive through a "process of healing", as Chris Alexander would say. In the presence of small and numerous squares in close proximity, the process evolved effectively. The squares prosper independently but they fit the whole conglomeration. Small they may individually be, but independently arranged, they are responsive to traditional habits and a sense of place. Quality of place is the essence of their survival.

The healing process is evident on the right bank in Paris. Rue de Rivoli, **18,** too, coalesced a flotilla of urban spaces surrounding the thrust of the new development. Rue de Rivoli started out as Napoleon Bonaparte's personal gesture. Feeling expansive, from his peoples' victories, he wished to demonstrate the peoples' glory. The Commission of the Artists

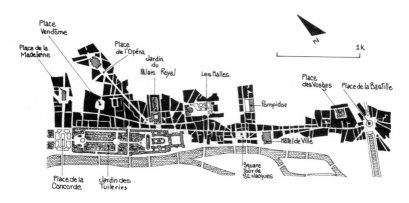

Figure 18. The Right Bank and rue de Rivoli Paris **31**

had drawn up a new plan for Paris in 1793. He began its realization. Until events took over.

Georges Haussmann came later. Directed to resume work by the third Emperor in 1850, even he was unable to finish despite his virtual absolute, authority. For at the end he was resisted successfully by the *bourgeois de Paris* who saw their old interests diminishing. To this day the urban vision of rue de Rivoli remains elusive. Nonetheless, rue de Rivoli, and Regent Street are archetypical offsprings of brave, fertile, confident imaginations. The work stands in defiance of the social upheavals of their day. We may apply contemporary social values all we like in criticism of Georgian priorities but we cannot discount the impact and beauty of their urban legacy. They remain still strong urban images reflecting the visions if not the conditions of their time.

The organizational machinations that set off rue de Rivoli and Regent Street reflect the planning antecedents of the Canadian imperial urban cultures. The main courses, Regent Street and rue de Rivoli, cut a swath through the old traditional cities. The surrounding areas responded. New patterns, flotillas of new and old squares and places, re-emerged. Interconnecting streets took on new and vital significance, for reasons different from their past uses. St. James's Square, Cavendish Square, Fitzroy Square, to name a few, surround Regent Street. Rue de Rivoli is flanked by place des Vosges, les Halles, place Vendôme and others. This intricate network of living, working spaces demonstrates the healing nature of the city. Some massive intrusions, resisted in their day, became the catalyst for renewed invigoration. Although we continue to enjoy their urban beauty now, we would recoil at such pervasive intrusions in our own neighbourhoods. And for all our sophisticated knowledge we are unable to emulate their qualities.

We appreciate the vision of the past so well, and so inadequate are we at emulating its urban beauty, we try to protect the past by isolating it from the present. At least in Paris they do. La Defence was the way they chose to do it. And it makes for an interesting comparison.

In Paris, recognizing the inevitability of massive modern intrusions, they have developed a separate enclave for modern development so the ugly modern towers do not defile the baroque quality of the traditional city. A virtual quarantine area has been established. It is the area la Defence. Bunched together in a bizarre ghetto at the end of the champs de Mars, the modern buildings are a marked contrast to the more rational traditional city. If ever the insanity of the modern era is in doubt, look at la Defence.

In London, there the modern buildings are scattered throughout the city. London's skyline resembles Dallas on the Thames more each day. And whatever shared vision there may have been is encroached upon by a wild and scattered vision of a market-place on the rampage.

Fortunately, we still respect the shared visions from the past, even if we have to fight tooth and nail to protect them from those marauders amongst us who see otherwise. For all the long forgotten difficulties, the Machiavellian intrigue and manipulation, the instigators of Regent Street and rue de Rivoli have handed down to us a treasured and shared vision. But we will not attain our own shared vision of urban space by hanging on to the past. The past shall become our future in a fractured sort of way unless we exercise the will to make it otherwise.

And what of a shared vision of urban space in Canada, now we have briefly aired the antecedents of the "founding" urban cultures. Can we look for appropriate images in Canada that demonstrate a vision of urban space to find out if such a thing exists? Whatever emerges could be useful for our own edification.

Regional creative energy is at an all time high in Canada. Pitted by narrow provincialism, reviled by aspiring cultured cliques, an indigenous architectural memory is waiting to emerge. It has the potential to be a generator of original designs. Yet in keeping with the Canadian condition it may remain forever and perennially potential.

Sophisticated trend-setters borrow interminably from international ideas, forgetting that to someone they are local. Where would the sophisticates of Toronto be if they could not scrump the apple of New York? Imagine what the world would have missed if the people of Trenchtown had had Venice and Berlin on their minds? Currying favour of the international set is still the favoured itinerary of the upwardly mobile architectural novitiate. And in Canada we are still unable to give credibility to an idea unless first it has come back to us from somewhere else. Notwithstanding, we can admire the achievements of our founding urban cultures and still see that we have progressed beyond our antecedents. Accordingly, a vision of Canadian urban space, tenuous as it may be, may yet be identifiable.

_33_

Inchoate as its form may be, there is a vision of urban space languishing somewhere, awaiting pollination. It can be found in the smaller cities, those that have not attracted the large developers and international trend-setters. Even in the larger cities there are sporadic instances where a shared vision has evidently defied the onslaught of international mindlessness.

Invariably the vision follows a determined purpose, responding to the habitual, the natural topography, or commerce. Downtown St. John's, Newfoundland, **19,** responds to all three. Common sense and usage determined the layout of the town. Habit protected its desirable characteristics from predatory development. The natural, spatially enclosed harbour is one of Canada's great urban spaces. Enclosed by green rock and the brittle forms of the built-up city the unfathomable depth of the smooth surface reflects the enclosing images back. The proportions are perfect. The harbour was the centre of St. John's source of wealth, in the past. The sloping city makes the harbour the urban focus from all the vantage points. Hopefully, the harbour will become the main source of wealth again some day.

St. John's and its harbour are impressive. More typically, however, the street layout determines the spatial ambience of the Canadian small city, not the dramatic combination of deep water and granite rock. Early military and railway surveys are evidence of the thinking behind many city plats. The flat

_34_

Figure 19.   St. John's Harbour Nfld from Signal Hill

topography of the prairie, the insistent work habits of the
surveyors and the railway engineers, often despite topography, make for a relentless uniformity. Their vision comes to
light like Roman fortified camps. And although the effect is
often tedium there are little glimpses of great beauty.

   One such Roman camp and glimpse of beauty is Charlottetown, **20,** laid out by Samuel Holland in 1765 and reminiscent of the 1733 Oglethorpe plan for Savannah, Georgia.

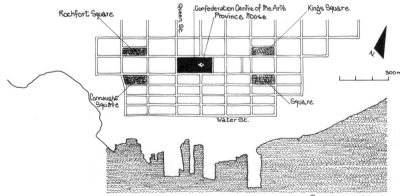

Figure 20.   Charlottetown Prince Edward Island.

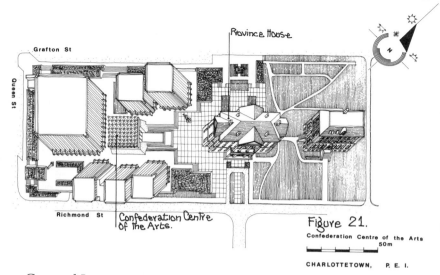

Figure 21.

Confederation Centre of the Arts
50m

CHARLOTTETOWN, P. E. I.

General James Oglethorpe derived his plan from the layout of
Roman castrums. And like the castrums there are spaces for
parks, symmetrically placed within the plat, of unbuilt blocks
planted with trees.

Charlottetown rises beyond tedium by virtue of its parks.
The layout is most pleasant, very easy to recognize. In the
centre is Province House. Contemporary downtown is an-
chored by the Province House and the Confederation Centre
of the Arts, **21.** Strolling the streets, inevitably the presence of
one of those symmetrically laid out parks, Province House or
the Centre come into view. The parks are demure and arbor-
ous. The centre abruptly changes the scale, for during the fes-
tival activity is hectic. Contrasting the demure residential
parks with the activity around the centre, Charlottetown
changes into a different place. Different from the railway town
it was. The military vision was one of unified order; democracy, such as it is, was not allowed. But no one would encroach
upon it now.

Saint John, New Brunswick, **22,** also has a Roman castrum layout. Centre, that is the original downtown, has
two complimentary urban places, Queen's Square and King's
Square, symmetrically arranged. The grand, dilapidated stock
of heritage buildings surround these squares in deference to
a past glory. They are clustered and the park-like squares
set them off.

Older buildings in the vicinity of City Hall have been

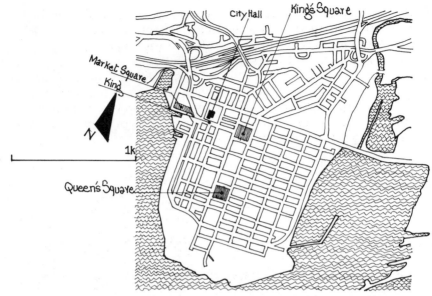

Figure 22. Saint John Centre N.B.

rejuvenated, where King Street comes down the hill from King's Square towards the water. The rejuvenation process has instilled the downtown with a new focus. Old and new are intermingled. Quite a vision. The new ostensibly accentuates

Figure 23. King Street, Saint John N.B.

the quality of the old. Still the new buildings display little grace or sensitivity. Designed in the current vogue (write-offs, tax dodges), they do little to enhance the town.

The older buildings, **23,** on the south side of the street are preserved to much better effect. Quite a telling contrast between the old and the new. Evidence that in Saint John the struggle for a shared vision is a toss-up between the quality of the old and the expediency of the new, a conflict not uncommon across the country.

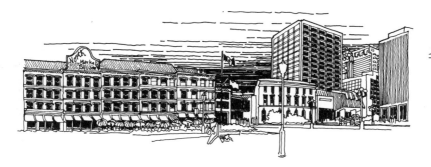

37

Figure 24.   Market Square   Saint John   N.B

The commercial focus of the renovated area is Market Square, **24.** The old commercial, marine oriented warehouses on the waterfront have been renovated into the usual tourist emporiums. A hotel has been added and, predictably, yet another convention centre. By default, this complex attracts attention. Perhaps it is meant to be the civic centre, a focus for "the people".

Renewal shows there is a lurking vision in the collective imagination of Saint John. That vision is badly bruised and threatened. Whatever past there was is in dire threat from the future, a future distorted by brutally conceived freeways ripping through the town—freeways going nowhere. Who knows what the city used to be? North of the centre, there in the valley where the train tracks run, the freeway has taken over. Is traffic that intense or have the numbers taken over again? Whatever was there, in any event, is lost. The freeway is pervasive. Moncton, the other industrial city in New Brunswick,

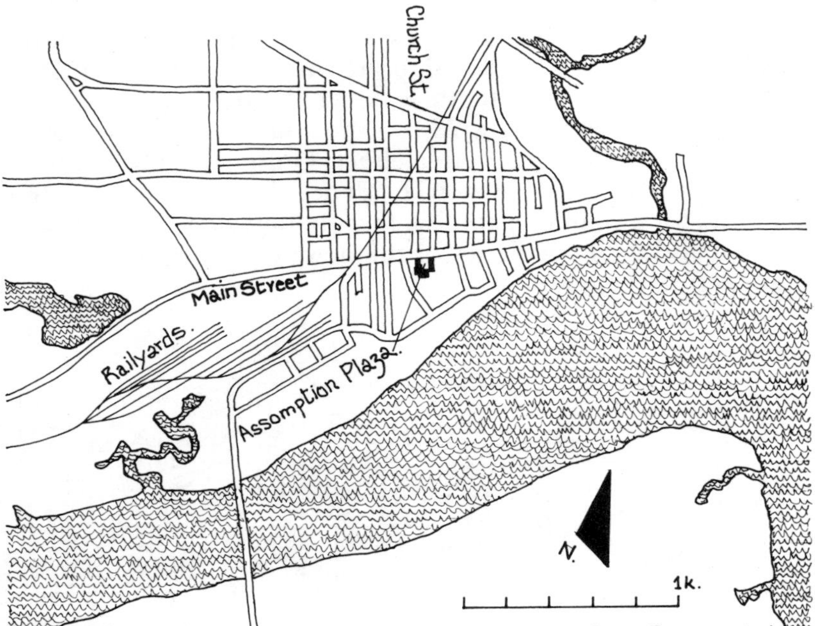

Figure 25.   Moncton   New Brunswick

38

is a railway town. Freeways in Moncton have been discretely muted. Neither is there the overbearing presence of modern development, at least not in the centre. The railway town layout is still evident and the street pattern adheres to the engineer's rectangular block plat, **25**. The severity of the rectangular layout is softened by the presence of the Petitcodiac River and Hall's Creek.

Modern development does not intrude so much, although it is there. Right in the middle of downtown is the Assomption plaza, **26** (one of the newest developments), on Main Street near the urban Oak Park. Unsuspecting visitors are pleasantly surprised walking down Main Street, coming across the plaza. The group of buildings comprising Assomption Plaza is a pleasantly situated, well laid out, functioning urban space effortlessly connected to the main street in the downtown.

The buildings on the plaza are Hôtel Beauséjour, Assomption Insurance offices and Moncton City Hall. Designed by Architects Four Ltd., Belanger & Blanchette, in 1986, it fits into the urban surroundings and gives to the city a sense of urban place.

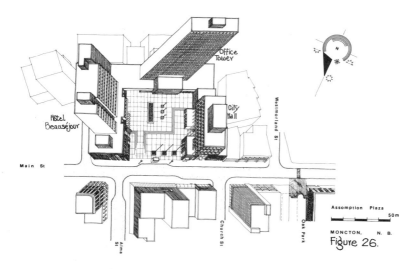

Figure 26.

That sense of urban place is a space right for Main Street, a natural flow from street to plaza. It could not have been better conceived. The new buildings surround a newly paved space, a place for people to rest or to conveniently enter the buildings. The proportions are pleasantly scaled in keeping with the old buildings on the other side of Main Street. The hotel and City Hall are marginally higher than the buildings of the street, well within its scale. The twenty-storey office tower is set back, enough to be neither looming nor overshadowing for the pedestrian. The surrounding facade surfaces complete the enclosure of the plaza. City Hall, Assomption Insurance offices and Hôtel Beauséjour all help to make the plaza. Architecturally, Acadian culture is alive and well.

The engineer's plat layout is not unique to Canada. Many cities on the North and South American continents follow the rectangular block plat, from La Paz to White Horse. The plat is the format for American urban living. No one in Europe speaks of going down the block. But here the military engineers, the surveyors and the realtors always came ahead to ensure the land was neatly carved up—ready to sell off. The Canadian city is not exceptional. Only that the plats are of a particularly formal type.

The street grid of the smaller Canadian city is so rigid, the purity of form is overwhelming. Calgary, Regina, Saskatoon, and all the myriad of little towns, have a grid street layout that is structurally gratifying. Regina, Saskatchewan, **27,**

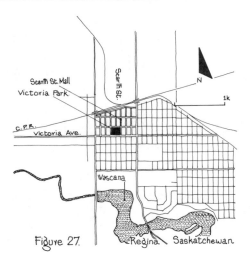

Figure 27.

follows so rigidly this formal pattern, Wascana Lake had to be flooded to introduce relief. In the middle of downtown more relief was needed and Victoria Park, **28,** was left in greenery. A betreed flat surface of open grass and trees, Victoria Park is replete with war memorial and memories. One memory that will not recede is marked by a small brass plaque, a reminder that Louis Riel was hung on this spot for sedition in 1885. The sense of the shared vision that inspired Victoria Park is illuminated by that modest little plaque and the importance of the buildings by which it is surrounded. It is quite beautiful.

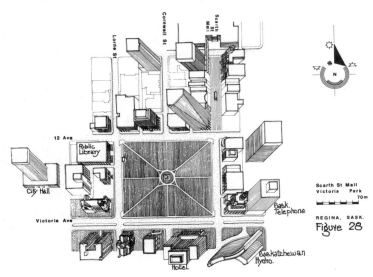

Scarth St Mall
Victoria   Park
70 m

REGINA, SASK.
Figure 28

The Canadian shared vision is the engineer's vision. Not surprisingly, therefore, it is authoritarian. The authority of the engineer was simply accepted. Accepted by the come-lately population, they would have been astounded had they been asked to participate in the formal design of the city they had just arrived in. The vision was a fait accompli before building started. Sharing the vision of the railway surveyor was a habit forced on the early settlers out of dire necessity. The people were so busy getting established, they had no time for schemes. The fine art of city design came later or sometimes not at all.

And the vision for Vancouver followed suit. Vancouver's shared vision has its roots in the railway engineer's dream too, **29.**

41

The story of the early spatial layout of Vancouver is fortu-itous. The platting of the streets is the genius of happen-stance. No one would have suspected the literal turn of the

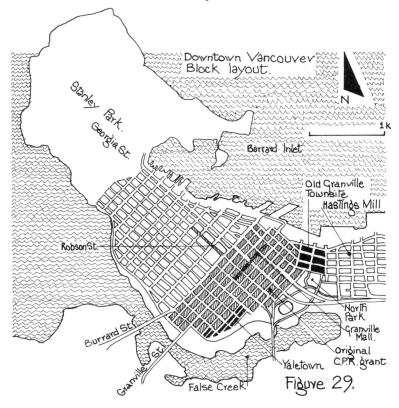

Figure 29.

streets when the original Hastings Mill plat was placed. Following the shore line the block layout gracefully turns from one townsite to the other, **29.**

The chronology goes something like this. Burrard Inlet was first settled in 1862. Hastings Mill community became established later. An enterprising saloon owner, Gassy Jack Deighton, capitalizing on the dredger thirst of the mill workers and the loggers, put down stakes just west of the settlement, next to the mill, still on the foreshore. His community became officially recognized in 1870 as Granville. The two embryonic communities were contiguous but their plats did not coincide. Still the two plats had to interconnect. Placed together the new street layout made a twist and turn. The miscalculation later became a most pleasant urban spatial twist.

The Canadian Pacific Railway came in 1886 and the city became Vancouver. The railway was enticed by a land grant which shows on the map as the hatched area between the two shore lines, False Creek and Burrard Inlet. Their land was platted under the direction of Lauchlan Alexander Hamilton, the CPR surveyor. He realigned the streets yet again and a third block proportion was introduced to the city. Yet another twist.

As the city was to be the railhead terminal a worker camp sprang up. On the north shore of False Creek their cabin layout became Yaletown. Then as commercial prosperity provided entrepreneurs with opportunity, expansion of the city west towards Stanley Park and yet another twist shape of block development was laid in place.

These unpremeditated, separate block formations ultimately contributed to the unpretentious genius of Vancouver's spatial ambience. The streets describe a vivid response, in the block layout, to the shore lines and the natural topography. No one could claim it was intentional, although no one can discount, either, the canny scots genius of Hamilton, in the manner with which he connected the two existing town sites, Granville and Hastings Mill. Vancouver's shared vision of urban space is a love triad, the people, the CPR and the land speculators. The effects of that twist continue to this day.

There are as many intriguing stories behind the spaces of every city in the country as there are cities. Vancouver's is but one. The railway rectangles of Regina, Charlottetown and Moncton and all the rest have become habitual. Maps cannot show the vital reality of the activity on the streets. Only

42

the vision held in every citizen's mind can characterize that.

But clearly the contemporary vision of the city has capitulated to the individual ego, relieved sporadically by occasional heritage distractions. Unless a case can be made for rampant traffic, separated ugly buildings and a general fractionated sense of city space, there is no dispute. But is there dispute? Professionals who should know better are locked in denial. Either they cannot see or they will not see the product of their disconnected efforts.

Perhaps the contemporary citizen enjoys all the noise and confusion, even if that proposition is hard to believe. Do we enjoy the shrill cacophony of urban noise? Maybe it is a form of relief from humdrum modern office jobs.

Still noise intrusion cannot be subjective. It can be rationalized but the numbers speak for themselves. Noise is very easy to measure. If there is any doubt that visually interrupted space is subjective, noise disturbance isn't. Take a look at the noise level readings in the appendices and make a comparison with the tolerances that accompany the readings. Chaotic noise alone is calamitous. Has this ever been considered in our shared vision?

43

Noise and visual chaos go hand in hand with the belief in the freedom to build how we please. That in itself is an inchoate vision. An attempt to pin down a contemporary shared vision on that count could, however, become a polemical mine field. We are not accustomed to visualizing a collective image of anything. Still we must be tiring of the perennial old worn out discomfort of the city. There is, alternatively, a grace and charm, an ease of accomplishment, when an undertaking is carried to the satisfaction of everyone.

Chaos is the result of a lack of urban vision. Freedom is the ability to respect those with whom we share responsibility. Freedom has nothing to do with anything goes. The current mirage of freedom blinds us to what our cities have turned into. We are too busy wallowing in apparitions of profit to see how unprofitable we have become.

Must our cities be devoted to escapist fun palaces and trivial spending places? Is the city to be committed eternally as a repository of boutiques, restaurants and pleasure domes of pop? Is the past of the previous precocious two decades to be the metaphor of our future, when we did it all for "the people"?

Will our vision always be usurped? Do our best intentions

always degenerate into fast food and commercialism, the apparitions of fast profit? Or are our cities to be places where we work constructively to accumulate genuine wealth?

Throughout history, people came together in the city as a place to generate wealth and to find a place to live and work. The coalescing motivation of the people of the city was to accumulate wealth and demonstrate it. Can we now put work back into the workplace: modern factories, clean production centres downtown, close and convenient to where we live? Can we redefine our definition of wealth, not as easy money, but as commitment? Does that fit our shared vision now? Perhaps we had better, soon, make up our minds.

For the portents are ominous. We are unsure of who we are! And when we know who we are, when we like ourselves enough, when we know what our cities are all about will we find the energy to reduce the noise and clutter.

Who we are in the city invariably comes down to who is building our city for us, who makes the profound decisions. Are we in control of our own urban environment? Indeed, even if we have a shared vision are we in a position to bring it about? We have already seen that the plat layout that started the city was often the work of an unsuspecting land surveyor or railway engineer. They would be amazed to see how lasting and pervasive their unpretentious work turned out to be. We participate to some extent, paying our taxes dutifully, attending those drawn-out public meetings. Many issues are addressed, few are dealt with. Our influence is limited. Civic-minded citizens have more pressing things to do, paying off their mortgage, bringing up the kids. And while we go about our daily business, there are people whose daily business it is to manipulate our urban environs. Who are these numerous anonymous moles deciding on our spaces for us?

They are developers, planners, architects and landscape architects. Every day, all day, they pore over their desks, immersed in concentration, making decisions on our behalf. They work in response to the guide-lines set up by elected representatives who represent our interests, or at least that is the conventional wisdom. But still their constant presence makes their influence more pervasive than the amateur citizen could ever be. And if the citizen does not have a clear understanding of what it is that makes their city flourish, the professionals do. And the professionals will mould the city in their own image.

Back in the days of Regent Street and rue de Rivoli the King and the Emperor had the vision; everyone else went along for the ride, at least for a while. Planning and redevelopment in those days, while not quite that simple, was straightforward. Accompanying much of the work on rue de Rivoli was the very necessary and unglamorous work of establishing an infrastructure of sewers and water supply. Land titles were medieval and complex; the merchants and traders were by no means enthralled by how their taxes were being spent. In the end, it was their will that prevailed. Still, the art of planning was much simpler, because not as many people were involved in the decision-making process.

Today the infrastructure is in place, although it is in dire need of attention. Flashy mega-projects distract us from our political responsibility to maintain the deteriorating stuff we cannot see. We take it for granted.

So now the crucial task is to coalesce the factions. We seem eminently capable of responding to crises when remedial action is too late, to a freeway or the imminent destruction of a heritage treasure. Yet on the long haul we let down our guard. We have trouble responding to events that come in casual sequence even though that is how the real creative building of the city works.

A heated debate over sharing a vision has just concluded in Vancouver. The debate exemplified our fractionate vision of our urban spaces and the buildings that surround them. A much-loved heritage building was at stake. Developers, architects, planners, as well as civic pressure groups, were drawn in. Demolition of the Georgia Medical Dental Building was the issue.

45

Figure 30.   Court House Square Vancouver, B.C.

Another most pleasing art deco building, similar in many ways to the Marine Building, the Georgia Medical Dental Building was designed by McCarter Nairn and Partners, Architects, in 1929. It occupied a very prominent site in the most significant urban space in the city, **30,** Court House Square. The Georgia Medical Dental Building can be seen on the left hand side under the arrow marking the 1929 building. The city was so used to seeing it there no other building can be countenanced in its place. Naturally, everyone, most everyone anyway, was up in arms, for traditionally it is a very successful design. Replete with terra-cotta figures, street level interest, warm and human facing materials, a well-scaled civic demeanour, the building was a veritable icon.

46

In place of the heritage Medical Dental Building is proposed a very fine new building designed by Paul Merrick, Architect Ltd—Cathedral Plaza. This is the source of the controversy.

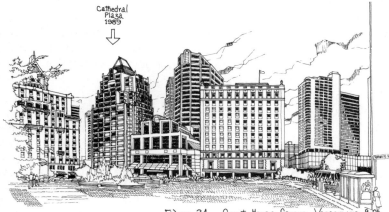

Figure 31. Court House Square Vancouver, B.C.

The proposed new building is superimposed on the sky line of Court House Square, **31,** as it will be built. City council approved demolition of the old building in July 1988. Is the new building superior to the heritage structure? Can we impose constraints on new development just because we have a quaint nostalgic memory? Cathedral Plaza is larger. But it is in better proportion with the surrounding buildings and open spaces. The roof of the new building is more elegant than the stump, flat roof of the heritage building. The details of Cathedral Plaza emulate the details of the building it replaces and the form of the Hotel Vancouver across the street. Given time, Cathedral Plaza can be just as much an asset to the urban spatial consistency of Court House Square as was the Georgia Medical Dental Building. Vancouver council made the right decision. We cannot depend on yesterday, for that is to deny our own creative abilities today.

Can both sides be right? Not according to Vancouver City Council. The old building was worthy but the new building is impending. Both add very much to the spatial quality of the square. The anti-demolitionists have every reason to fear a new structure judging by the incongruous hulk next door, the Bank of Hong Kong, completed in 1987. Indeed why was there no indignation when the old Devonshire Hotel was blown up to be replaced by that one. But the designs of new Cathedral Plaza look good so far. Let's hope the next phase in the development doesn't break the architect's heart.

47

Still the urban battles rage on. Visions of urban space conflict, the antithesis of sharing. In Montreal a similar battle was engaged. The New Sherbrooke Apartments across the street have been demolished to expand the museum. Where is a shared value when a perfectly serviceable apartment building is replaced to accommodate a museum extension? But it isn't bricks and mortar that is at stake, it is the vision in our minds of how we wish to live.

As the battles rage we must yet bear this in mind. A shared vision of urban space must still coalesce around one fertile visionary idea. Even in this day of egalitarian administration the civic leader who grasps the significance of urban beauty, who inspires the people's support will have a tremendous influence on the outcome of the process. That person will have the ability to coalesce the various factions whose interests affect the city and persuade them of the benefits. The benefits go way beyond convenience or aesthetic delight.

Describing the origins of railway layouts, devising civic arguments to salvage dubious heritage monuments in Montreal or any other city, hardly describes a citizenry committed to participating in, and understanding, their urban environment. Indeed, defining a shared vision of urban space in that way is an exercise after the fact. We all share a vision of the city as it exists. That is simply demonstrating an acquired habit. Struggling for heritage conservation and using the street block layout is accepting and sharing a vision of someone from the past. We do not need to exercise our imaginations, nor do we need to find courage. If anything, acquiescing merely reinforces the image of our squalid misdirection.

The age of kings and emperors was simpler than today. Squalor was a part of the city; many people lived in degrading conditions; they didn't count. Decision-making was a one way process. Consensus was achieved, not by discussion, but by the quaint faith in the last vestiges of the infallibility and divine right of kings. What the king wanted was hard to challenge, although in the days of Nash and Haussmann even that rough-shod consensus was on the wane.

We have transferred a naive faith in the divine rights of kings into an equally naive faith in the divine right of the voter. Voters, evidently, are no more prescient than kings. Politics may indeed be governed by perceptions but events can still prove our judgment to be wrong. Have we misplaced that faith? Many people in history struggled, suffered and gave their lives that we, today, may exercise freedom. We are free from autocratic, arbitrary rule, we can express our choice by voting. And what do we do? After strong and faithful people from the past sacrificed and struggled to gain us freedom, what do we do? While the smart set tries to be Italian, we go shopping.

Truly, the collectively expressed vision of a free voting public today manifests its form in plastic shopping malls, restaurants and heritage bunkers. Is that really what we want? Probably not. Still there is no evidence to suggest a better vision will materialize from our good intentions.

The outcome of the revolution of the sixties was to involve the people. Yet, as planners refine the process of participation committees, they become more manipulative. How often do participation meetings degenerate into information meetings? Too often to be admitted. Who participates? Usually perennial committee goers. We end up preaching to the converted. And in any case, how can we possibly corral all the unformed ideas people have of their city? Most people don't give a damn and stay away from participation in droves

So how does a shared vision of urban space come about? Is it an esoteric socio-cultural phenomenon? Obviously not, but neither is it distilled from solicited, accumulated answers to questionnaires sent out by city hall. Not that peoples' answers have no value, of course they do. Question—do you like views? Answer, a resounding yeah. Question—do you

_48_

like safe streets? Answer, again yeah. This exercise has no form and can only result in a large collection of conflicting answers.

The contemporary city is the living image of our system, liberal democracy. People respond accordingly. The late C. B. Macpherson, in his book *The Life and Times of Liberal Democracy*, described how we see ourselves as objects, separate from one another, commodities that can be sold. In his words: 'Market Maketh Man'. The present generic city characterizes this conception of ourselves perfectly. Every artifact and individual of the city is conceived, built and exists separately. There is no common cause. So how can we expect people to respond with conviction about something from which they feel alienated? And how can we expect them to participate in a mature and responsible manner while this system is in place? So until a change occurs we have to make do.

And one way we make do is to rely on others to take responsibility—let the other guy do it.

And so a collective vision becomes a series of values held by an elite group. And that elite group will exercise leadership. Leadership gives direction to the conflicting requirements of diverse public opinion, demonstrates needful priorities and places in perspective the unfocused direction of the city. But what of consensus? Obviously autocratic edicts of any kind would be laughed out of consideration in our free-wheeling civic discussion process. And, why try for a consensus anyway? Instead, a collective vision should be inclusive enough to hold together, allowing for even the most disparate values. The vision should be spatial, flexible and textured allowing for all reasonable values to be included.

Furthermore, lacking the assumed infallibility of kings and emperors the elite group cannot just impose its vision. Even if that were possible it would not work. For without the consent of a responsible public nothing works, even if a responsible public have no shared vision. It is, therefore, incumbent upon the elite to inspire, educate and gently cajole. Civic leadership is needed, not ideological but inspirational, visionary leadership. For without consent no vision can last, or even come about.

Idealism, participation and dedication are at the root. Who but a small group of idealists would, or could, take the trouble to carry such a notion through? Then obviously the question arises, if a shared vision of urban space is the domain

49

of an elite group, how does participation fit in? Who are these people who share visions of urban space? Well, in fact those people can be anyone. Their only fitness for participation is commitment and interest. Anyone who is interested to take the trouble, those who are interested enough to inform themselves of their city can participate. It is up to us all to be vocal.

The vision starts as a germ in, perhaps, one or two people's minds. Fertilized by necessity, circumstance and an understanding of civic pride in history, the vision is ephemeral by nature. The germ grows in other people's minds. The elite group proselytizes. The idea matures. And as it passes from one to the others it expands. Time passes, everyone participates. Ultimately, it blossoms into something we can all express. Then it is ours.

50

3

Imagining Urban Space

Victoria Square is in a state of animated disruption. Harbour- *51*
front belies its promoted excitement. Without doubt Cathedral Plaza is a better building for Court House Square
(Vancouver, B. C.). than the old Georgia Medical Dental
Building. The old building may be a heritage treasure but
what tangible values do we share to help us make the right
decision? Upon what reasonable foundation can we decide
the fate of either Victoria Square or Court House Square?
Will the outcomes hinge, by default, upon obscure hiero-
glyphics, masquerading as economic benefits, in the books of
soi-disant accountants? Values that are ephemeral at best;
benefits for a few, latent debt for the rest of us.
     Only an extremely naive person would believe anything
but a cultural rebirth will begin to address the complexities
and wayward economics of the modern city. What possible
credibility does a discussion on urban spatial merits have
when the market dictates everything? Where is the evidence
that the market works? Is it, too, just an arbitrary myth, taken
on faith to fill the voids of our imaginations and courage?
How can a rational discourse take place against irrational,
unproven, messianic expectations? How can we shift the discussion from more and more of the same thing that seeks
solutions in the root causes of the symptoms?
     If we cannot see what is before our very eyes, if we are
unwilling to admit the city is unworkable, if we persist in applying the same rules to a deteriorating condition, we will
continue to run around in circles. If we will not admit failure,
how will we break the vicious circle? That is the status quo and
only a complete change in attitudes will provoke an awakening.
     One way to break the status quo is to read and un-

derstand the medium of the city. Look at the chaos, listen to it. Respond to the magnitude of the effects. Recognize that the significant part of the environment is what we see and hear in the city's urban spaces. Read the message in those fractionated urban spaces. Sensitize ourselves to the message and we will recognize the current state. Recognition is a grand step forward.

Urban space has always been a major preoccupation of Western culture. Art, power and religion have found expression through the enclosure of space. We judge the past on the lasting images of the spaces of urban architecture. From the Greeks to the Romans, from Gothic Cathedrals to baroque urban spaces, our culture in the past expanded its reach through space. Space expresses vision.

We fail, unfortunately, to judge ourselves by the same criteria. Something has happened in modern times. Enclosure of space has become an expediency. Space is a commodity to trade. That must change. And we can start by accepting the significance of urban space.

Cubist painters were the last to explore a vision of space in this era. Apologists for modern architecture will protest this statement vehemently. Surely, however, no sensitive observer would claim modern shopping malls and gallerias, those dissonant, glass-topped, architectural voids—the epitome of *haute-vulgarité,* to be worth emulating as examples of our best effort at enclosing space. Surely we can do better than that?

The cubists explored beyond the Renaissance vision of space perspective. The cubists struggled on the flat surface to demonstrate time-lapses of movement. They introduced the fourth dimension, time. Paintings by the cubists expressed and exposed the multifarious dimensions: up, down, beyond and the time consumed to see it all simultaneously. They wanted us to see all sides of their subject at once, to view the three dimensions in one glance, as though all sides were in view without the intervening time-lapse of moving around the subject. They put the fourth dimension of time onto their canvases and into our minds.

The cubists' depiction of time influenced our visual perceptions and ultimately percolated into general circulation— notably through advertising techniques. But, and this is no surprise, only the superficial visual effects came through on a general architectural level. Time was left out and space was left out. The impact of their images remained on the two-dimensional surface.

Time applied to space demands that we imagine the interweaving of inner and outer space as a Mobius curve of connection. That is recursion. Recursion is a succession of returns. Space also is a succession of returns. Urban space recursion occurs when complex spaces are interwoven between complex architectural shapes, the outside and the inside of the building. Space in time applies to urban space when we can imagine buildings to be solid forms and spaces to be positive forms. Positive forms of space are interwoven into the solid forms of the buildings. Inside, outside is continuous. Spaces are connected to spaces, solids are connected to solids, spaces are connected to solids in a continuous experience in time. Time connects the solid and positive forms and the mind's eye retains the accumulated image.

53

Time and recursion introduce the element of duration. Duration is time extended into the mind's eye. This is where intuition takes over from scientific reasoning. In urban architectural space, duration in time is the lapse of moments that occur as we move and let our eye absorb the many facets and surfaces of the enclosure we are experiencing. The ability we have to store images in our mind's eye and then relate them together as a composition is duration in the context of urban architecture.

Time has been forgotten in contemporary architecture and duration is not yet understood. Time, the fourth dimension, has had surprisingly little effect on contemporary urban spaces. If anything, urban architecture has become even more two-dimensional. Modern architectural space, despite erudite protestations, is an organization of the flat surfaces. Stratified office building floors, stratified apartment floors, the long stratified level of the shopping plaza mall have taken on the stratification of ancient, geological outcroppings, anything but a response to the exciting revelations of the cubist, time-conscious, artists. Only sporadically did the artists of modern architecture find isolated opportunities to express time and space.

Indeed in our fervid preoccupation with the division of tasks we ignored Hermann Minkowski when he wrote in 1908, "Space by itself and time by itself are doomed to fade away into mere shadows, and only a kind of union of the two will preserve an independent reality".

For the great majority of urban circumstances time and space went blank. Contemporary architecture became marooned in slices of flats three metres high. Architectural facades relegated flat reflective surfaces to mocking back images of ourselves in a Warholesque mimic, retreating from recognition; bland, silly and inconsequential. Architecture became the victim of the market mentality. The city is regnant with the damage.

We have failed to imagine the potential of urban space because we do not understand duration in architecture. We no longer see the street; we just see doorways. We no longer see facades in relationship to one another, we only see single buildings. How we desensitized ourselves to the environment of space is not difficult to understand. The proposed addition to the Montreal Museum of Fine Arts, for example, evokes an urban spatial issue that makes the point. Montreal exemplifies many such debates, as do, across the country, Toronto and Vancouver.

The museum is on Sherbrooke Street. Evidently the addition will disrupt the habitual vision the city is accustomed to. The vision is of a street with buildings lined continuously along it. Locally, it is called "the Sherbrooke Wall". The preservation of the Sherbrooke Wall and the spatial ambience of the street is very important to many people. Important enough to rouse their ire when it is threatened. The architectural form of the proposed museum addition threatened the alignment of the wall. The new addition will gut the apartment but retain the facade.

How can that be? Is it more expensive to align with the rest of the buildings? If we value the spatial effect of Sherbrooke Street; if we understand the history of Western space; if we were watching the cubists, how could we allow the view of Sherbrooke Street to be threatened? The answer is quite simple: we have forgotten how to imagine urban space.

Imagining urban space is not a unique cultural phenomenon. Nor is it unique to historic periods. But it is clearly not on the contemporary agenda. There is evidence to suggest circumstance moulds regional perceptions of space. Weather, opportunity, behavioural circumstances have played a role, if only limited in scope. So imagining urban space may not be entirely at the mercy of market happenstance. Even if, for now, the realization of it may be. Gaile McGregor offers an interesting insight into how Canadians perceive urban space.

54

She contends we have acquired environmentally induced perceptions different from the Europeans and the Americans. Her thesis is described in her book *The Wacousta Syndrome.*

Her conclusions were formed after she studied the works of Canadian artists, painters and writers. She read in the medium of Canadian art a distinct perception of space. According to McGregor we do not share the grand regal sense of space that demonstrates the power of kings that was the way with Europeans. Nor do we share the vast open spaces vision with the Americans. The Canadian sense of space is moulded by the hostile climate. In contrast to spatially expansive Americans, who have exploited a warmer and friendlier climate, we face the barrens with foreboding. Where they see the warm sun setting on the distant plains, we see the broken ice on the flooding rivers. When the Americans sally forth to seek their fortunes, Canadians venture heroically, well-clad, long enough to glean sustenance, then return safely to their cabins.

McGregor interprets the message of Canadian art. We have acquired our sense of space, not as conventional wisdom would have us believe from wide open spaces, but from a dire sense of foreboding towards the hostile environment. Canadians sense space as safety, close, warm and enclosing. A sense that comes from an acute awareness of the shivering bleakness outside. When we express our uninhibited selves our urban spaces reflect a tenor of cabin fever. She postulates an interesting theory. It should provoke a new look at ourselves and encourage us to rethink an architectonic idiom more relevant to our needs than imported pre-digested images from abroad.

Is the Sherbrooke wall threatened because we have placed expediency above our deeper feelings? Did the original builders of the wall respond subliminally to the sense of enclosure out of climatic conditioning? Were they just emulating the narrow tight streets of Europe, from whence they came? Or, are we missing a unique opportunity here to reinforce our connections with our urban past?

The theory is intriguing. But urban space can be understood more fundamentally. Indeed a simple way of understanding space can be explained by adapting a high school science experiment. Something familiar to us all.

The model describing tangible fields of force surrounding magnets in proximity to one another is an analogy that can be applied to buildings in close proximity to one another. Ur-

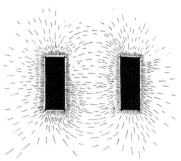

Figure 32. Magnetic Field of Influence

ban space can be imagined by visualizing, or pretending if you like, a field of spatial influence emanating from the buildings.

Remember the science experiment. Not the one when the rats got out and ate our lunches. The one that demonstrates the lines of magnetic influence surrounding a magnet, or the lines of magnetic flux. The teacher sprinkled fine iron filings on a plain sheet of paper. Two magnets were placed in the iron filings on the paper. The iron filings assumed a pattern. What had been invisible lines of magnetic flux surrounding the magnets became visibly apparent in the pattern of the iron filings. The pattern described lines of magnetic influence as though stresses were flowing from one pole to the other. Stress lines of influence appeared to emanate from the magnets. Lines of influence were distinctly flowing from one magnet to the other, **32.** There appears to be a surrounding aura associated with each magnet. The space between the magnets appeared to be a distortion of the field relating to both magnets. One magnet by itself evokes one pattern. Two magnets evoke another pattern and their proximity to one another evokes yet another pattern in between.

Imagine that buildings are magnets. The surrounding imaginary magnetic field of a building follows the same lines of influence, in a visual sense, as a magnet. The lines of influence emanating from the buildings draw our attention. The magnetic lines converge from one building to another. The intensity of their drawing power depends upon the proximity of other objects in the urban setting. It depends on the propinquity of the buildings.

For convenience, imagine space as volume filled with the auras emanating from the solid forms of the buildings and surfaces that enclose the urban space. The auras, or penumbras, are imaginary lines of influence emanating from each building, similar to the magnetic lines of influence from a magnet. Imagine buildings projecting auras or penumbras into urban space. The penumbra of each building intermingles and fills the volume. Space is the volume filled with these intermingling penumbras. The penumbras can be designed so that each building complements the other. The beauty of the urban space comes out of the artistry with which the building forms project their penumbras.

Imagine fields of influence emanating from the buildings aligned on the Sherbrooke Wall. The lines converge in the manner shown in figure **33**. The shapes of the building sections in this sketch are general, not representative of a specific part of Sherbrooke Street. The lines of influence respond to the shapes and patterns of the aligned buildings. The details of the buildings, the overhangs, the bay windows shape the field of influence correspondingly. Lines of influence run between facades in such a way that they are modified by the propinquity of the buildings. The lines converge in the spaces between and fill the volume. Their shape and direction is transformed by contact with other buildings' penumbras emanating from surrounding facades.

57

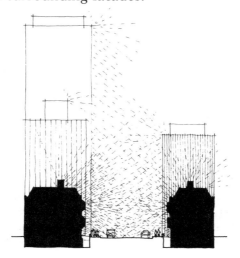

Figure 33. Imaginary Field of Influence.

Visual and spatial points of Attraction
Figure 34.

Buildings have volume and project a field of influence
that can fill a space. But even the occurrence of intersecting
lines on the surface of a building can be a point of visual focus,
effected by the lines of influence. Intersecting lines make
shapes that modify the penumbras of the buildings. Two lines
converging can attract visual attention, **34.** And urban space is
an amalgam of these complex visual influences, whether they
are columns, cornices, masonry lines or door frames.

Space comes about from a composite of these lines,
forms, voids, applied patterns and suspended patterns. All
the physical elements that come together to make up the
visual effect of the street bear on our view and by association
on urban space. To be effective they must be composed; that
is architecture. And they must be composed to evoke a subliminal response. When they are composed with an understanding of their effect there is architectural harmony.

Shapes and patterns on facades have interrelating influences. This is where the cubists' vision of the fourth dimension of space is relevant. Cubists expressed space on the two-
dimensional surface by superimposing planes upon each
other. Cubists could depict the fourth dimension on their canvas. They achieved this by showing all sides on one surface by
ingeniously distorting the image. The architect cannot show
all sides on one facade, obviously. He must introduce the
fourth dimension therefore by recursion and visual image re-
tention. With this opportunity he can enrich the design of the
facades by combining the phenomenal effect of recursion and
the mind's eye ability to retain images. And with the mind's
eye we can accumulate images and interpret them as on one
composition. Thus we can say we have eyes in the back of our
heads. We can, in effect, see forward and behind simultaneously. This is the effect of well-designed architecture on urban space. If the treatment of the facade is subtle, architecture
will reflect the simultaneous occurrence of time and space.

58

Advertising artists have used these techniques for a long time. They know how to seduce the pocket book by wooing the eye. They learnt well from the early theorists. Lazlo Moholy-Nagy's book, *Vision in Motion,* and Gyorgy Kepes book, *Language of Vision,* articulated the theory of the magnetic field of space analogy and visual stimuli in their research into the subliminal sense of four-dimensional visual space.

Does this analogy help to widen our angle of vision? Does it put eyes in the back of our heads so we can comprehend space in volume rather than as single snap shots? If we can change our imagination from seeing isolated single objects to seeing the lines of influence that flow between the objects, then we have discovered a sense of space, urban space. Can we now discern patterns coming from the corner of our eyes? Does it help us to see that the shapes and patterns of a building on one side of the street may affect the way we see another building on the other side of the street?

59

This is no mystery, but it is a concept strange to the modern mind. Inanimate urban objects are not imbued with supernatural forces, of course. The lines of influence flow in our imagination only. Shirley Maclaine has no place in the mythology of the Canadian urban space. The theory, together with its model, the magnets, merely describes a simple technique for visualizing urban space. It is described only to help in imagining and visualizing lines of influence in urban space as the best way to view the city as space, to help us see the city as more than a collection of buildings occupying chunks of land but rather as a living organism full of ever-changing animated substance related by fields of influence.

Stretch the imagination, without stretching credulity, and visualize the attracting lines of influence emanating from facade to facade. It can be an invigorating experience, an easy way to imagine urban space.

For when all is said and done the city is space. All the happenings, events, smells, noises, experiences we associate with the city occur in, and come from, urban space. Urban space, city space, is a series of views that open as we move. The city is holes between buildings. "Though clay may be moulded into a vase, the essence of the vase is the emptiness within it", said Lao-Tzu. The holes between the buildings is the essence of urban space in the same way that the emptiness of the vase is the essence of the vase. Each is filled with those imaginative, potentially malleable lines of influence, or flux.

We have been conditioned to see the city as buildings, lined up on the street, sometimes dumped haphazardly on open spaces, and we fail to see the possibilities presented by the spaces between. We have acquired a habit of looking at the buildings while ignoring the spaces. Indeed, often those spaces between the buildings are hazardous streets, leftover chunks of land, after-thoughts made into parks, perhaps even the cows of Saint Bank pasture, for want of something better to use them for. Not very interesting and accountably ignorable.

We have slipped into the habit of not seeing space because we really do not know how to explain what space is. Is it a hole? Is it nothing? Can we sell it? Can we buy it? If we cannot eat it, we ignore it!

_60_

But space is the city.

Public urban space is volume, a living substance. Urban space is volume enclosed by building faces and paved surfaces. And volume is the measure of capacity of civic plazas, streets, walkways, back lanes, parking lots and landscaping. The building faces and pavements are the surfaces with which the volume is enclosed.

The treatment of the vertical and horizontal surfaces, the paving and the facades, effects the feeling of the space. Light reflection, shade, materials, plants and textures combine to set up how we react.

Urban space is given life by the artistry with which the enclosing surfaces are treated. The quality of urban space is determined by the surfaces with which it is enclosed. The manner in which volume is articulated by the building walls, the paved surfaces and landscaped areas, determines the quality of the urban space. The relationships of the elements of architecture that surround and contribute, set up the ambience. The shape of the volume and the way it has been moulded, the intensity, direction, nature and velocity of the movement within the volume all conspire to move our urban perceptions. That is what urban space is!

In Chapter five, six significant urban spaces are illustrated and analysed. Many aspects of these urban spaces are discussed. One important part of the illustrations is the effect the lines of spatial influence have when applied to real circumstances. However, not all significant urban spaces are as well composed as those illustrated in chapter five. There are many places where the art of imagining urban space has been disregarded, or threatened by disregard. An analysis of four such spaces follows. The first example is the combined urban space, Dominion Square and place du Canada.

Dominion Square and place du Canada in Montreal demonstrate our recent loss of ability to imagine urban space. These two spaces demonstrate how carelessly we treat the city and its spaces simply because we fail to exercise our imaginations before rushing ahead with new development. The planners in Montreal simply didn't bother to imagine the effect those few new developments would have on the traditional image of that very important place in the city.

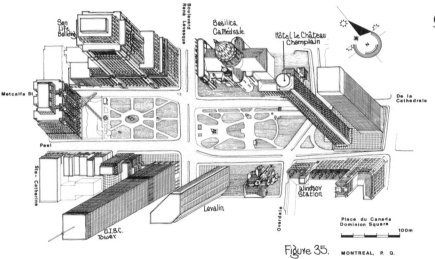

61

Figure 35. MONTREAL, P. Q.

Dominion Square and place du Canada, Montreal, **35,** are interconnected, the two read as one space. Named separately, divided by a maleficent throughway, the spaces have defaulted into one amorphous mass. They have defaulted into an amorphous mass because in the early sixties the appearance of the urban space, before many of the older buildings were replaced, was obviously not appreciated by later developers. Whatever happened to our sense of space in the modern era happened with a vengeance in these two potentially beautiful spaces..

Dominion Square and place du Canada, is a neglected space much like Victoria Square. The old surrounding buildings withstand the graceless omnipotence of the new arrogant

towers tenuously. Combined, the two spaces are living dem-
onstrations of the evolving phases of the city. Old graceful
buildings constructed around the turn of the century are
devoured. The old sense of neighbourliness that existed
between urban buildings in the city has been relegated to
obscurity. Dominion Square, place du Canada and Victoria
Square are a living record of the procession of events.

The combined spaces are surrounded by about sixteen
buildings. Rotating clockwise from the north-west enclosing
face of Dominion Square, **35,** they are, the Dominion Square-
building, a parking garage, the Sun Life Building, the Cathedral, the Cardinal's palace, the Federal Office Building, Hôtel
le Château Champlain, a church, the Lavalin Building, the
Canadian Imperial Bank of Commerce, an office building and
a group of small commercial buildings. The construction
work, in front of the Dominion Square-building on Dominion
Square, was completed in late 1987 as an underground parking facility.

Some of the new towers are emblems of corporate pres-
tige, enjoying a privileged address. Nevertheless the space
has an ambience of fractured, incompleteness, a separateness.
For an urban space of such national significance its appearance belies its importance. *Je me souviens* says the collective

62

Figure 36 Dominion Square & Place du Canada looking North.

consciousness of Québec, but indeed they have forgotten. Dominion Square and place du Canada more than any in the city are indications Montreal puts no value in the significance of urban beauty.

Once there was a magnificent beauty to Dominion Square, **36;** remnants show today. At one time someone carried in their mind's eye an imagined vision of what the space would be. In the summer the trees and the grass are still a haven of pedestrian charm. The canopy of leaves deflects the sun and dampens the din of traffic. The massive presence of the Sun Life Building remains familiar. The front facade is a theatre set of chiaroscuro. Drama is happening to the light reflected off the grey facade surface. The columns and the window indentations catch the sunlight, yet never is the massive form exerted. Sun Life is the last remaining building on those spaces that displays a form at all. The others are remote, separate, accentuating dismembered space.   *63*

Whoever carried that beginning vision in his mind's eye had a sense of space no longer held in the contemporary planning agenda. Clearly, using the imagination for visualizing urban space in Montreal is no longer encouraged. There is no indication, currently, that there is an imagined vision of urban space in anyone's mind's eye to direct Dominion Square and place du Canada into a completed urban spatial form. The contrary is the case.

The spaces are a place in transition. Yet again a newer city is emerging. Emerging, fractionate 1980s architectural forms are breaking up the space, dominating the traditional ambience and disrupting the view. The ambience is so unhappy even the new buildings show to disadvantage. And the ensuing distracting agglomeration demonstrates the importance of imagining a vision of urban space before impetuously pushing on with development.

Currently place du Canada, **37,** presents a spatial quandary for the perceptive city lover. The space is surrounded by unrelated buildings that do little to enhance the space. They make no profound contribution to the surroundings. Indeed they detract from it. The space left by these disparate and separated buildings is interrupted and discontinuous.

The four heritage buildings, the Cathedral, the Cardinal's palace, the station and the church, are diminished by the new buildings' presence—the Canadian Imperial Bank of Commerce, on Dominion Square is so preponderant.

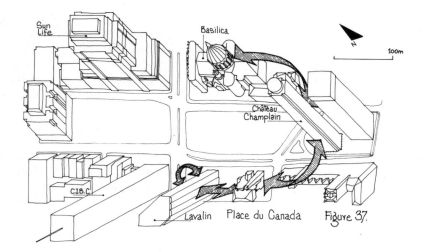

Lavalin   Place du Canada   Figure 37.

Arrows, in **37** and **38,** draw attention to the spatial cavities between the spindle-like tower of the Hôtel Château Champlain and the Lavalin Building and the gap between the Hôtel and the Cathedral. Another arrow points out the incongruous corner siting of the Lavalin Building. Indecisive corners such as these allow, metaphorically speaking, space to slip out as if a spigot is opened. The arrows show how the visual magnetic fields of influence surrounding the buildings are not strong enough to bridge the gaps in between. The fields of influence are inconclusive, contributing nothing to the sense of urban place enclosure.

Figure. 38. Place du Canada Looking South.

More development will occur in place du Canada. And because of that there is a strong need for an imagined vision. Many of the old and smaller commercial buildings surrounding Dominion Square will be gone soon. The holes revealed in **37** and **38** can be healed if the potential developments are integrated by a mind's eye vision, indeed a shared vision of urban space. This is not a matter of imposing additional expenses on the developers. No extra expense is involved. It requires only careful and imaginative planning. There are no practical reasons why this should not be done. The spatial presence of Dominion Square could be maintained. The south-east quarter of place du Canada could be completed. Some semblance of urban space could be retrieved.

Dominion Square and place du Canada were obviously _65_ conceived as a comprehensive mind's eye vision at once. The spaces are ceremonial centres of importance. Their very names imply national significance. Their current condition is a living example, nevertheless, of how easily we forget the values that originally inspired the vision. They show how careless we have become in planning new developments. Wit and cunning can help us not a bit if we do not use our imagination.

Phillips Square, east from Dominion Square on St. Catherine Street is another urban space in Montreal, once beautiful, now in danger. This is the second example of urban space that is disregarded.

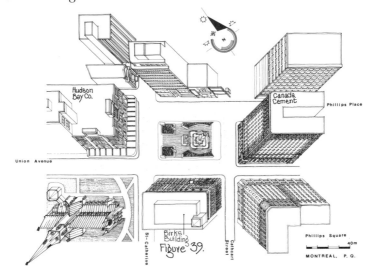

Figure 39.

Phillips Square, **39,** demonstrates four aspects of good urban space. First, space in Phillips Square was unequivocally conceived by the original planners as an intentional mind's eye image. The square is not an expediently retrieved piece of space left out of the overall plan. It is there as an integral part of the street system. Secondly, the street layout absorbs the spatial surface as a part of the functioning purpose of the city. Third, the enclosing facades follow an alignment making the extremities of the space immediately recognizable. And, finally, the human scale of Phillips Square is compatible with the commercial purpose of its enclosing buildings.

Evidently imagining, in the mind's eye, the effect of an urban space was an accepted planning function when this part of Montreal was laid out. Apparently pedestrian movement was the primary purpose, hence the square provides an appropriate pause in the street layout. A sense of pleasure is experienced when walking down St. Catherine Street as suddenly Phillips Square opens up. The square is a clearly defined pause, no ambiguities. It has a central theme, the statue. It has a central rest area and the surrounding streets are narrow enough that the pedestrian does not feel threatened by the traffic.

The square is an integral and functioning part of Montreal's street layout. Robert Allsopp, contrasting a Toronto urban space with the traditional urban spaces in Europe, writes, "The difference between these places and Trinity Square Park is that they are not vehicles of escape but integral and vital parts of their cities. They are extensions of the buildings which surround them and of the streets which connect into them." His comment applies appropriately to Phillips Square.

Four streets converge on the space smoothly. The street pattern is enhanced by its presence. The square de-marked inside the street pavement is a place to display an important civic statue. Pedestrians may congregate and rest on that place undisturbed by traffic. It is a plaza-like opening in the built up sequence of the buildings, an opportunity to emphasize entrances and window displays.

Like the Sherbrooke Wall the buildings surrounding Phillips Square define the space. The facades formally follow the rectangular shape of the square. The alignment of the facades has been respected by successive developments. The lines of spatial influence emanating from the surfaces are well composed and fill the volume. Each facade is individually designed and recognizable, yet continuity between surfaces enhances the tranquil ambience.

Phillips Square's human scale is in keeping with street widths and building heights. Yet imminent development could threaten this balanced scale and an evaluation of height to width should be made before tower buildings are started. The parking lot on the east side does little to encourage and the tacky movie house on the corner is hardly enhancing. Perhaps the scale and ambience of the connecting streets will ensure a traditional continuity for future development, unless a very large land assembly changes the scale in a massive way. The heritage significance of the better preserved buildings should encourage compatibility of scale of the new and potential neighbours.

67

Phillips Square is a rare and valuable urban form for city space in Canada and it is threatened. The main characteristics demonstrate the four major elements of urban space, i.e., intention, integration, alignment and scale.

Heritage architecture is one of many aspects of the square that should be held of most value for it determines the present architectural ambience. One heritage building on the square is the retail store and head offices of Henry Birks and Sons. A very beautiful building, it could be a model to guide newer development. Hopefully, the changes made to the Birks presence in Vancouver in 1973 will not be repeated in Phillips Square in Montreal.

The Birks store in Vancouver is on an urban space that demonstrates the way urban space is retrieved from the castrum type street layout rather than as space that evolved out of intentional mind's eye image.

The store shares a site with an office tower. The complex is called the Vancouver Centre, on the south-east corner of Granville and Georgia Streets. The space at the intersection is the third example and it demonstrates how not-so-satisfactory urban space is created out of necessity because it is the only opportunity available in an area short on supply.

The corner, **40,** is the emotional epicentre of the city. That, however, was apparently not important when the space was first conceived. In fact, it was originally intended to be an intersection of two main roadways, just another crossroad on the railway engineer's grid. No one had in their mind's eye an image of a spatial pause on the street. The intersection has

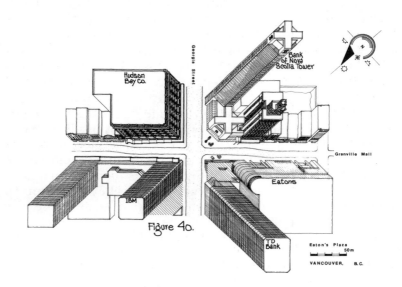

Figure 40.

been retrieved from what is still an inhospitable pedestrian urban environment.

The south-west corner of the intersection is dissected by Eaton's Plaza. In the typical modern manner the plaza cuts the corner off to no purpose. As a pedestrian pause, most of the day, there is no sun. The paved area is essentially superfluous to the pedestrian space already provided on the Mall. Traffic noise is unpleasantly pervasive. The plaza is not an integrated part of the spatial network in that area, as Robert Allsopp explains, rather it is an imposed afterthought.

Until the mid-seventies the buildings surrounding the intersection were vintage 1910. In that era facade alignment was accepted, indeed subliminally so. Only The Bay, on the north east corner, and the Vancouver Block, one building in from the south east corner remain from that era. These buildings follow the street alignment and to a limited extent show off the shape of the streets on which they face. Across Georgia Street Birk's new store does not enclose the street, indeed it is shaped in defiance of the street alignment. And the scale of the Vancouver Centre Tower is all-consuming. It even outscales the TD Tower.

Eaton's plaza is an afterthought expeditiously retrieved after the street grid plan had been conceived. It is one of those anomalies that come from the bonus granting system (a developer is granted additional revenue producing floor space in return for a public amenity). Planters, paving, lamp posts, an information kiosk and a clock are sited attempts to ameliorate the overbearing distractions of traffic and unrelated buiding forms. The attempts have not worked. The pervasive ambience at the intersection does not say "urban space, pause, relax".

A critical look at that corner plaza demonstrates the need for bold intentionally imagined visions of space in the mind's eye when planning large scale downtown projects, for although the Eaton's Centre is large and pervasive it is not an example of bold and imaginative urban planning.

Both Phillips Square and Eaton's Plaza have relatively small ground area surfaces. They are 91 by 77 paces and 133 by 104 paces respectively including the street paving. The tallest building over-looking Phillips Square is 42 metres, in a proportion of 0.4 of the longest dimension. The TD tower over-looking Eaton's Plaza is 117 metres, in a proportion of 1.7 of the longest dimension.

69

Dominion Square and place du Canada are grander: the ground surface of the latter two is 4.5 hectares combined. The highest building, the Canadian Imperial Bank of Commerce, on Dominion Square is in the order of 187 metres, in a proportion of almost 1.0 to the longest dimension of Dominion Square.

The heights of the buildings on all the urban spaces mentioned in the preceding paragraphs vary considerably. Comparisons yield no normative standards. Still the height/width proportions are within a one-to-one relationship when taking into account average heights and ground dimensions (Phillips Square is somewhat less). And although the spaces vary considerably in apparent and actual size, so far as height/width proportion go, as public urban space, they work.

The height/width proportion of Olympic Plaza, **41,** Calgary, does not work. It is even larger than Dominion Square and place du Canada and it is right in the centre of the city, which is much smaller than Montreal's.

To imagine interrelating lines of influence filling this space is not easy, it is so vast. The ground surface is about two hectares. City Hall Plaza, Steven Avenue Mall and the surrounding streets add even more, if included. The heights of immediately surrounding buildings vary, but seldom reach thirty metres.

Figure 41. Olympic Plaza Calgary Alta

70

High-rise office towers of downtown Calgary loom imminent in the distance, erupting like huge basaltic masses, occupying the sky line, unrelieved by a blank sky. Their downward
thrust, their repeated tower shapes offer no relief as they
dive into the broken streets at ground level. The surrounding
rigid block layout is flat: streets and vertical towers, no
variation.

The plaza is like a shallow bowl of space carved out of
their middle. The immediately surrounding buildings, the
bank and the church are virtually unnoticeable. They are
overpowered by the scale. Prickly in appearance, the distant
towers don't even enclose the space. They haphazardly surround it. Within the shallow bowl, whatever imaginary lines of
spatial influence the towers may generate stray loosely apart
as they sweep away from the centre. Everything seems so vast,
so un-urban!

Olympic Plaza is so unrelieved, bereft of defined smaller
increments, it is hard to read as an urban space at all.

It would work better if it were made up of small micro-
spaces each identified within their own right but still interwoven in the whole. Micro-spaces need not be demonstrative,
just little areas of seating, planting or a different pattern
of paving.

Olympic Plaza is without proportion. The sweep upwards
from the vast open surface to the high of the middle distance
could be a very compelling form, somewhat Mayan, somewhat

of the plains, if the surrounding buildings defined its shape more precisely.

But there is no scale. Stand on the flat surface of the plaza, look in any direction, the surrounding space recedes to nowhere. Building facades are isolated, fragmented, so distant that any sense of enclosure is pure speculation. There is no building alignment recognizable in the sense of the Sherbrooke Wall or the surrounding buildings of Phillips Square or even the potential of place du Canada. The surrounding buildings are remote from the plaza surface. The towers of Calgary are a series of vistas constantly moving away. This is not a public urban plaza at all; this is a civic revocation.

71

4
The Principle of Sustained Interest

Architecture fills the same role in city building as the press in legislation. The design and the treatment of architectural detailing in public urban spaces describes the motives behind the design of the facades. The medium of urban architecture is potent, far more so than the conventional media of newspapers and television in affecting our subliminal psyche. Unlike conventional media, however, when the architecture of the city speaks it says what it means.

What it says is being ignored. Robert Allsopp again writes of Trinity Square Park, Toronto, "It demonstrates, as well as any, the current confused state of the art of public urban space design and our inability to control the forces which shape our modern cities. But it is only a park. It was commissioned and is owned by a Parks and Recreation Department that clings to a nineteenth century view of a park as an escape from the city—when what was needed was a bit of Barcelona's Ramblas or Placa Reial, a touch of Venice's St. Marks, Rome's Piazza Navona, Montreal's place Jacques Cartier. . . ."

Escape from the city is evident in more places than Trinity Park. What started out in the early seventies as a movement to bring the city back to the people has turned into flimflam: restaurants, boutiques and malls everywhere, a material escape. Instead of defining the city by some useful purpose we have been seduced by glossy presentations. The design professionals have abrogated their responsibility for the design of urban spaces to the pretty picture renderers. Restaurants, boutiques and malls can be very stimulating, of course, but to have them used as a substitute for substantive development eventually defeats the purpose.

The principle of sustained interest is a response to that

flimflam. Confronting the emerging shallow nature of urban architecture, the principle recognizes the economic impossibility of retail continuity on every street: to line every street and space with shops and restaurants. Neither can architects continue to rely upon imported trends, gleaned from the glossy international architectural pulp press to dress up their renderings, for they seldom meet the needs of a particular circumstance. So the principle reveals the elements of architecture that are relevant to the design of good urban spaces to ensure interest at street level in those places left blank between the restaurants and pretty store fronts.

The principle of sustained interest states that the surfaces enclosing a public urban space must have a lasting and stimulating quality. The architecture of those surfaces must hold our interest for a sustained period of time and it must stimulate our intellect. The principle addresses the effects of the architectural detailing of building facades and the effect of activity in the space. Interrelationships between the architectural elements on facades and activities must be appropriate to the urban space. It requires that the elements within the enclosed space respond as a whole, aesthetically and environmentally.

73

The Elements of Urban Space.

PLASTIQUE	PALETTE	EMPLOI
Ambience	Materials	Ritual
Propinquity	Colour Texture	Grain Motion
Scale	Permeability	
Surface Chiaroscuro		
Metre-Proportion		
Enclosure-Vista-View		
Icon		

Within an urban space the composition of architectural details must be treated in a manner that evokes the observer's capacity to probe beyond his immediate recognition. The architectural nuances that comprise the space-enclosing surfaces should sustain the interest of the observer, stimulating his intellect beyond first glance, into a search for more complex architectural elements. The interest of the observer should be invigorated by the designer's wit and skills, provoking a search, penetrating a rich and permeable outer facade, into the intricacies of the detailed patterns beyond the immediate front surface. The architecture of public urban spaces must catch and keep the eye of the interested spectator.

Architecture and landscape architecture are the fundamental ingredients of public urban space. In elementary form, then, urban space is designed detail by detail, building up a patina of quality until, co-ordinated, the whole adds up to more than the sum of the parts.

Fundamental, "The Elements of Urban Space" are listed above (p. 73). Essential details are recalled to the urban designer in the same way that the cockpit check-list reminds the pilot of an aeroplane before take off. The list is reduced to elementary headings. Three main headings describing the essential characteristic, are *Plastique,* describing volume, the moulding and shaping of form, *Palette,* describes materials used to construct and modify surfaces that enclose volume and *Emploi,* signifying the activities that occur within the volume.

74

Plastique

Ambience. Ambience describes the surroundings, the total volume of urban space. In this context it describes the overall quality and the subliminal effect of the urban surroundings on our psyche. It describes the overall composition of the public urban space, the accumulated effect of all the elements in the starting program that ultimately add up to something called urban space. Landscaping, trees, absorbing surfaces contribute a soft ambience to an urban volume. Material surfaces contribute visual ambience.

Noise disruption detracts from the ambience. Noise level readings are shown in appendix I. Appendix II lists tolerances. Comparisons of the two provide revealing conclusions. Traffic, especially construction trucks gearing up and down, is the major cause of noise in urban spaces. Amplification and noise resonance caused by the shape and the impermeable resonating surface materials are elements that most affect ambience.

Propinquity. Propinquity describes nearness, proximity and the closeness of the building surfaces. The way buildings relate to one another and the way their facades describe the urban space is the subject of propinquity. Buildings, or solid forms, and the interstices between the buildings, or positive forms of space, set up relationships. Public urban space is the positive form of space and it is filled with the imaginary lines of influence emanating from the buildings. Propinquity is a direct outcome of the lines of influence that fill the volume of the urban space.

Until recently the aphorism, form follows function, has been a very popular motivator of modern building form. Taking this dictum to heart, the modern architect moulded the building exterior to follow the function inside. He forgot how the building facade contributes to the urban space outside. For this reason urban spaces constructed in the modern era are seldom recognizable because modern architects became so concerned with following internal functions they neglected the shape of the external functions, namely the articulation of the outside surrounding urban space. And the appreciation of propinquity in space remained dormant.

75

In the urban setting space is a function. An important function is that the shape of the outer surfaces of the building describes the shape of surrounding public urban space to which it contributes. Buildings contiguous to one another set up spaces between that respond to the accumulation of all the buildings. This is propinquity. Recognizing the effect propinquity has on public urban space and the shapes between the buildings is a Gestalt.

Scale. Scale represents dimensions in proportion to a unit of measure. The unit of measure in public urban space is human form, what else can it possibly be?

There is also the matter of scale of buildings in relationships. Public urban space surrounded by tall buildings evinces three levels of scale: the street level where the human dimensions apply to the pedestrian activities; the middle level, that part of the building's solid form between the street level stories and the roof, that is for the neighbour's outlook; and the roof contributing to the skyline of the city. Roofs and middles are discretionary but street level can only be measured by the human form.

Tower buildings should be integrated into existing urban streets in response to the three levels. Towers can add to the scale of public urban space, as is demonstrated in the siting of L'Edifice Price on rue Sainte-Anne in Québec City, figure **42**. Urban space does not depend on low buildings. L'Edifice Price is a high-rise office building of its day. It is significantly higher than the neighbouring buildings. But the scale between the tower and the neighbours has been mitigated by

Figure 42. Hôtel Clarendon & Edifice Price   Québec | | P.Q.

artful design. The scale relationship of the tower with Hôtel Clarendon and the cottage on the other side is an example of an urban relationship that can be exploited in other urban settings.

The acceptable height of downtown buildings keeps going up. In 1967 Toronto's TD Centre was the tallest in the country, now there are many towers taller. There are virtually no engineering constraints to stop the rising climb. So the only scale criterion we have is the human form. Even the tallest, the most densely populated project, can be divided into manageable proportions on a human scale vis-à-vis the three levels of scale.

Surface. Surface is exteriority, the interface between the solid form of the building and the positive form of space. It is that imperceptible film where solid changes to void. Surfaces are the planes that enclose space. They are the basic elements of public urban space. The surfaces of the buildings, the facades, describe the surrounding vertical enclosures of the public urban space. The surfaces of the streets, lanes and sidewalks, the pavements, the street and plaza paving, the lawns and landscaping, and sometimes the overhead covering surfaces, describe the horizontal enclosure and give direction to the spaces.

Surfaces may be angled to set off an effect. Surfaces can be inclined to modify apparent scale. Setting them at angles modifies the light-reflecting qualities, modifies the microclimate and compensates for disadvantaged orientation. Perspective can be varied and distorted by surface angle. The vertical surfaces can be set at angles to modify the scale of the surrounding buildings.

The manner in which surfaces are treated conditions us to use urban space in a predetermined way. We habitually treat roadways with blacktop and we habitually relinquish road surface to single-use vehicular traffic. We treat modern facades with plain, bland materials and habitually we ignore them. We accept lawns as a place to slow our movement and a pattern of paving to direct our movement. By design we need not follow habit. Relating surfaces to one another is spatial design and that element is crucial to the composition of space.

Napoleon was aware of this. He was concerned about the design of public urban space when he ordered the building of rue de Rivoli, **18,** in Paris. He was so concerned he set up what is probably the first build-to line, **43,** an official design control to direct the alignment of buildings. The control drawing set up a pattern, a continuous street front, and co-ordinated the separate and individual acts of development into the cohesive spatial composition.

77

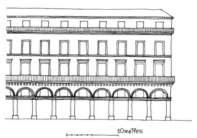

The official design control drawing, Rue de Rivoli Figure 43.

Chiaroscuro. Chiaroscuro is the treatment of light and shade. A technique commonly referred to in painting as the artful use of light to mould surfaces, the manner in which shade reveals the nuances of an uneven surface. The painter defines his forms in colour, light and shade. The flat surface of the painter's canvas can be brought into apparent relief by alternating light and shade, thus extenuating the depth of the rendered image.

Chiaroscuro in urban architecture exploits the light and shade reflecting off a building facade. Chiaroscuro is a technique for sculpting the surface of a building by contrasting

Figure 44. Old City Hall, Toronto

light and shade. It helps sustain the interest of the observer as light changes according to the time of day, time of year and the conditions of weather. The light and shade on the facade varies as the sun follows its ecliptic. The architectural details, columns, window recesses, architraves, cornices all project shadows on the building facade. The designer must exploit the varying shadows stimulating movement on a static surface.

Traditional and heritage architecture is highly valued for many reasons but chiaroscuro is the most evident. The way the heritage facade reflects the light, the way a heritage facade is reflected by contemporary glass surfaces, imbues an otherwise commonplace experience with vitality and a lasting interest. Contrast the facade of the Old City Hall in Toronto, **44,** with the new, **73.** The details, the texture and the form of the old building changes throughout the day as the arrises catch the moving light and reinterpret our recognition.

Contemporary architecture has not exploited this quality. The flat monosyllabic detailing of the contemporary office building adds little in the way of sustaining interest unless it has a surface reflecting the surrounding buildings.

Metre-Proportion. Metre is our sense of poetic rhythm. On the building surface it is the measure of intervals between vertical, indeed also horizontal, lines and forms, columns, pilasters, windows and doors.

78

Proportion is our sense of comparing separate parts. The parts are the architectural characteristics and measurements of the facades. Architectural characteristics are seen in terms of correlations and corollaries. Measurements are seen in terms of ratios. That is metre.

Metre and proportion are closely related in the context of visual design. The rhythmic metre of a row of windows may also set up a measure of proportion of the spaces between the windows. Metre and proportion can relate facades of separate buildings by correlating the rhythms and details of one surface to another. Architectural characteristics may rhyme thus contributing to the wholeness of urban space.

Enclosure-Vista-View. Enclosure is the quality of completed space. Enclosure defines our sense of place. Enclosure is the feeling we experience when surfaces wrap around our angle of sight.

_79_

Enclosure surfaces interrupt our line of vision. Our optic senses gauge distance, relating close surfaces to distant surfaces, relating surfaces in our direct line of vision with surfaces in our peripheral vision. The summation of this is the sensual experience of enclosed urban space.

Figure 45.   Quebec P. Q.

Vista is perspective seen through the interstices of the enclosing surfaces. It is the long and distant prospect, of a distant mountain range or the city skyline. Or it may be a wide panorama of the whole skyline, **45,** like that seen from Lévis across the St. Lawrence to Québec City.

View is the visual survey of the closeness we see around us. In the context of urban space view should be defined differently from vista. View is the close prospect of the buildings in the immediate vicinity, the enclosed urban space. Vista is the long shot.

Halifax is one of the few jurisdictions that have defined view requirement in law. Twelve defined vistas are described

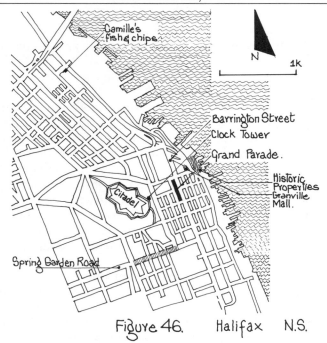

Figure 46.   Halifax   N.S.

as seen from the citadel, **46,** above the town. The vistas of
Dartmouth, George Island and the harbour are deemed to be
so significant, corridors of low building height are projected
within the downtown business district to preserve the line of
sight. Cones of vision protecting these vistas are placed in the
city development guide-lines. No tall building can be erected
within these sight lines.

Vistas from the citadel in Halifax also incorporate views.
In the distant vista is the harbour and Dartmouth and in the
foreground is the view of the Civic Clock Tower, **47.**

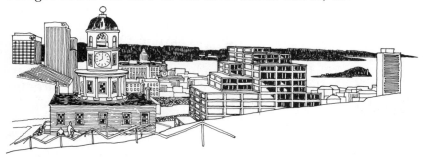

Figure 47.   Halifax   N.S.

Figure 48. Toronto from Ward Island

Views and vistas are important planning criteria. Sketch- **81**
es do no justice to either. Four views and vistas in Toronto
and Vancouver are shown in simple graphics: the vista of
Toronto skyline as seen from Ward island, **48;** the vista of
Vancouver's skyline and the mountains as seen from Fairview
slopes, **49;** the view of downtown Toronto, close to Roy
Thompson Hall and the Royal Alex, as seen from the corner
of John Street, **50;** and **51** is a close up view of Vancouver
from the Devonian Park on Georgia Street. Both **50** and **51**
are not usually seen on the picture post cards.

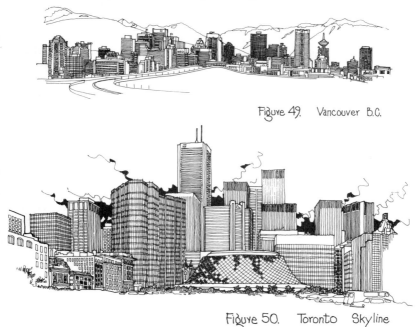

Figure 49. Vancouver B.C.

Figure 50. Toronto Skyline

Figure 51. Vancouver, B.C.

Close views of enclosed public urban spaces are as pleasant to contemplate as the distant vistas. Architecturally, it is impossible for every window to enjoy a vista no matter how ubiquitous it may be. Therefore we should come to recognize and value the view of an enclosed urban space as equal in value to a vista.

Icon. Icon represents values and motives in visual, material form: the semiology of architecture. Icon is the incarnation of ourselves. It is the graphic, actual presentation, in architectural form, of values. The representation of icon on the face of our built environment is a give away of what is important to us. Icon is that part of the medium of urban architecture that will tell us what we value. Are we really interested in what we have euphemistically dubbed culture or are we irrevocably wound up in numbers?

Architecture is the mother of the arts. Icon is the video screen. Architecture gives birth to the arts then continues to supports them. Tapestries, sculpture, painting all need architecture. Theatre, ballet and recitals (even open air performances) need architecture to perform in. But what of the architecture itself. Have we cobbled it together so quickly, so cheaply, to swank because we've spent so much on pictures? Have we gerry-built the thing just so we can dress up to see the ballet?

To the statement often used in the development business, on time, on budget, icon asks the question: "What is on time? What is on budget?" And the semiotics of icon decries the answers.

That concludes explanations under the heading of *Plastique.* The list of headings under *Palette* represent the range of substances with which we construct architectural images. The *Palette* contains the material elements of the building facade evident visually and to the tactile senses.

Palette

Materials. Materials can be anything. All the stuff we have at our disposal. All the product of industry that is directed toward buildings. Indeed, even found items that are not directed toward buildings, like driftwood, recycled rubbish, flotsam and jetsam. In the conventional world material usually manifests as stone, masonry, terracotta, metal, plastic, glass and concrete—technological hyle. There is an endless proliferation of material stuff, in the competitive industrial city, much of it the same, packaged differently for marketing purposes.

Yet the combinations and computations of the way we relate material to material is the key to the artistry of urban design. Materials relate in ways that are best seen in urban spaces where old and new buildings are sited contiguously. The Marine Building, **52**, Vancouver, is sited on an intersection, **11**, surrounded by contemporary architecture. The facade of the Marine Building is richly detailed in the art-deco style, coloured glazed clay tiles and earth coloured masonry. The advantageous contrast of the art-deco to modern curtain walls enhances the comprehensive ambience of the urban space. Indeed the modern stuff could not survive without it.

83

Figure 52. Marine Building Vancouver B.C.

Historically, architecture has been most revered when building materials have been used sparely. Where economy of use has been the prime purpose of design, architecture is at its best. Economy, artful, skillful craftsmanship and engineering has always produced the most beautiful architecture.

Colour. Sensation is produced on the eye by rays of light. Colour is a sensory perception; it holds no material property of its own. Perception depends on colour relationships. Complementary colours, red/green, yellow/blue violet, and blue/yellow orange, enhance one another. Primary hues are more vivid when placed in surrounding fields of complementaries. Colour theory is science; colour application is an art. Perceived colour is a response to light and weather conditions, point of view and cultural conditioning. Materials have no inherent colour properties of their own.

Personal mood swings, often attributed to colour, are learned (socially conditioned), they are not innate responses. People may differ in responses to colour according to the ages of the respondents. Young children tend to prefer bright primary colours, whereas older people prefer more subdued colours.

Colour is relevant only in terms of relationships within the urban environment. Proportionately it has a dramatic psychological effect far beyond its application. Colour as surface application may only be a few millimetres deep yet the response it evokes can be heard for miles.

The time has come to take the mystery out of colour, for colour is only colour insofar as it can effectively modulate our perception of space; otherwise it is benign. It is another element that can add richness to our lives. We owe a responsibility to ourselves to use it. And it is most certainly a necessary relief from what has become the official mark of city life: the interminable sequence of concrete and glass, drab in the cold, drab in the heat, drab in the rain and snow.

The subject of colour is wide. Other publications penetrate its science in depth. For practical purposes only two aspects of colour may be considered as a part of this discussion on urban space. The two are, natural colour inherent in materials, brick, wood etc. and chemical colour. (Colour in landscape is another matter.) Natural colour in materials, wood, stone, brick, clay etc., evince a texture that causes colour to change depending upon the angle from which it is viewed. Chemical colour is generally applied to surfaces in paint form.

Paint now available on the market is colour-fast in almost all primary hues. Fastness of colour is no longer a reason to avoid its use. Sunlight reflects off colour surfaces and affects it differently from various orientations.

Canada is unique in that it is the only northern country, with the possible exception of Finland, that does not display vivid colour in its urban environment. Perhaps it is the result of some dire reflections on our experience, what Gaile McGregor is telling us in her Wacousta theory.

Exceptional in Canada is Newfoundland. The vivid display of colour on the streets of St. John's, New Gower Street, **53,** is quaintly extraordinary to the Canadian fear of bright open colour fields. The ink line drawing, **53,** gives no indication of what colour is like in St. John's. But if we can just for a moment assume an eidetic pose and think of the richest possible hues in the most varied combinations, that is the effect of colour on the streets of St. John's.

85

Texture. Texture is the arrangement of small constituent parts. It is most evident in this context on building facades as surface substance, small scale, rough and touchable. Surface texture is a quality that evokes a response to the tactile sense, and a visual response in small, complicated detailed architectural arrises and facets. Texture is the rough feel of

Figure 53. New Gower St. St. John's

Entrance Door   Place d'Armes
Figure 54.

masonry and the coarse thread of heavy fabric. Complicated terracotta details such as the architrave surrounding the doors to the old Quebec Bank, **54,** on place d'Armes appeals to our sense of texture. Texture, more than any other quality, makes urban architecture attractive, especially heritage architecture. Texture is the one design element most lacking in contemporary urban architecture.

Permeability. Permeability is the quality of surface that allows penetration, saturation and diffusion of our visual attention. Permeability is the attention absorption factor. A quality of surface that attracts our attention beyond first glance: a very important part of the principle of sustained interest.

Multi-layered and apparently multi-layered surfaces have a visual depth that draws our attention beyond top surface. Designed properly, this could be an attractive urban design element. Depth of surface, light attracting and reflecting, shadow creating contribute to this effect. This form of surface treatment exercises the wit and humour of the designer. Does the surface detail draw our attention beyond first glance? Is it possible to retain the details of the facade without straining our attention?

On the other hand, bland innocuous surface treatment inherent in much commercial architecture encourages us to take buildings for granted. When we have seen one we have seen them all. At that point we have forsaken ingenuity and we have lost a sense of ecstasy in city life. Permeability is one of many small architectural elements that may give it back to us.

That concludes explanations under the heading of *Palette.*

The list of headings under *Emploi* represent the employment of space and the occupations and activities that transpire within its volume. Emploi is the reminder of the activities that will ultimately circumscribe the manner in which the public space is perceived.

Emploi

Ritual. Ritual in this context is activity in the secular sense. Ritual may be the simple meeting of two friends or it may be a glorious parade. It may be a commercial activity or it may be a small-scale occurrence.

Urban spaces can be simple urban squares or busy intersections. In any event, the activities that transpire within the volume of the space are determined by the shape of the space, the links with which it is connected to the surrounding urban fabric and the purpose to which it is directed.

Grain. Grain is the mix of traffic types that move across the space. If the space is used by many types of movement, say trucks, buses, automobiles, bicycles, wheelchairs and pedestrians, the grain is coarse. If the space is used for only one type of movement, say pedestrians, the grain is fine. The nature, viscosity and consistency of the traffic activity is referred to as the grain.

Motion. Motion is the activity of moving, obviously, and in this context differs from ritual insofar as it is purposefully directed and does not pause or stop within the space. Movement of direction, intensity, volume and velocity of activity and traffic are motion under this definition.

Modern city traffic patterns have consistently been guided by the philosophy of separation, that is by keeping vehicles off the same surface as pedestrians. Surfaces of motion are generally graded as arterial roads, feeder roads, local roads and walkways.

The "Plus 15" elevated pedestrian system in Calgary is a separation of pedestrian from street and traffic. This separation is achieved by means of pedestrian bridges overpassing the traffic streets from building to building. Inside the buildings there are dedicated, connecting, pedestrian corridors. There are elevated parks, some open, some enclosed. Devonian Gardens is enclosed. The system remains incomplete in 1988 and, as a viable system of movement, enthusiasm for it has apparently waned.

87

Boulevards are being revived as a means to humanize arterial routes. The great tree-lined, military parade route, so awe inspiring of the regal empires, defined on either side by double-rowed linden trees is thought to be a way of treating the modern inner city throughway now that freeways have been rejected by the public. In Ottawa such a tree-lined ceremonial route is proposed to circle the downtown. For Quay Street West on Harbourfront, Toronto, wishful thinking planners propose a boulevard with double-lined trees, hoping it will hide the persistence of the traffic. Georgia Street, Vancouver from the west, is to be treated in the same way. Vancouver calls it greening the downtown. These are makeover, cosmetic jobs proposed to make do with an unsatisfactory environmental condition, hardly relevant to the mitigation of deleterious effects of motion.

Superficial treatment of this nature makes little difference. The cafés, the linden trees, the *boulevardiers,* are the futile dreams of other days. They cannot survive the vapid stench, the malevolent presence, the horrific din of modern, relentless, city traffic. The only way we are going to reclaim our cities from the traffic, short of universal public transit, is to accept the reduced velocity and volume caused by congestion.

Within city spaces a new approach is becoming recognized. This is the matrix approach, or as it is called in Holland where it was first demonstrated, the *Woonerf* method. The method proposes the sharing of the street surface. In Utrecht 200 streets were designated as "shared streets". This meant that all modes of traffic shared those streets. The ensuing congestion reduced vehicular velocity thus improving safety. The street scale became more recognizable and the single overriding priority of traffic was tempered to fit into the fabric of the pedestrian city. Could the emotionally volatile North American public cope with the ensuing frustration?

Another approach has been tried in Vancouver. Traffic was purposely relegated to a second priority in the planning of the False Creek neighbourhood in Vancouver in the mid-seventies. Parking, street widths, traffic access was designed with the expectation that public transit would take priority. Although comprehensive transit is still a long way off, complaints about parking do arise but no undue inconvenience to movement or safety has transpired. Dire predictions simply did not materialize.

Close to False Creek a form of the *Woonerf* system has

been in operation, successfully, for some time. One of the many desirable and attractive aspects of the Granville Island urban development has been the laid-back traffic mix. Purposely slow-moving traffic mixes with pedestrians to reduce the velocity of vehicles, and to reduce the ensuing danger to pedestrians while they are shopping on the island. The coarse-grain mix on Granville Island demonstrates how successfully traffic congestion inhibits fast-moving vehicles from endangering and disturbing people on foot.

This concludes the explanation of the headings under "The Elements of Urban Space". The previous paragraphs outline, along with some personal proselytizing, a simple set of principles for the design of public urban spaces. It is not definitive but it transcends a dependence on ephemeral trends without being doctrinaire. **89**

Public urban space results from team effort, no one list from one mind can possibly cover all the intricate exigencies. The list nevertheless opens the discussion of urban space away and beyond the current restricting architectural debate over styles. For whether a facade is detailed with a key stone or classic portico has been, by virtue of the overstatement, relegated to a fad. Architecture is too important for that.

Fads are rife and far too dominating in architecture. Architectural style has, until the next great era of creative thought rescues us from current myopia, become quite irrelevant. If Mrs. Smith wants her French Provincial covered wagon she will have it. If Mr. Jones wants his Dallas Cowboys cardboard mansion with Go-Go boot gate posts, why not? We have the resources, technical and financial. We are a pluralistic society and if Disney is the order of the day who is to argue. The style is quite unimportant. Whatever we want we can have and there's plenty of talent waiting to do it.

The current architectural debate, revival of modernism, constructivism, de-constructivism, eclecticism, all the persistent, imported, second hand, arcane status symbols cease to be relevant in the face of principles. Dogma is too exclusive and if the truth could be admitted, conducting an architectural practice under such dogmatic conditions is about as intellectually stimulating as running a corner grocer's store. Style is one thing but commitment is another. Really, if our cities are to survive the people who commission architects are going to have to make more responsible decisions. Do they want architects who spend their time marketing their services, with trendy pictures void of content, or do they want architects who commit their time to architecture? There is a world of difference; marketing is one way of looking at the city, urban architecture is quite another.

Commitment does not involve style. Style has to do with taste and when we choose our taste by civic responsibility style may or may not be appropriate. Still, committed architects have other priorities on their agenda. Anyone can design for style.

We are not the only age to enjoy a pluralism of architectural styles. The intellectual debate of the Victorian era was a constant schismatic rift between the classic and Gothic revivals. Unfortunately for us, however, the debate is not on such an intellectual level. The architectural pluralism of today is divided, roughly, into two camps. On the one side is a sort of virulent pipe-itis, hi-tech, dear to the hearts of a naive enclave of professionals who believe it represents the cutting edge of technology. On the other, is a soft, indulgent interpretation of historic forms, keystones and clock towers, propagated by a glitterati with pretensions of European sophistication.

The utility of architecture would be much better served if both sides adopted the principle of sustained interest at the expense of their charismatic illusory images. Charismatic styles are not so enveloping as to preclude questioning our sense of building relationships, a sense of neighbourhood, in the urban environment. Urban architecture must now move into the post-literate domain of space and relationships. The great architectural challenge has become the creation of public urban space.

So far the challenge remains unnoticed. The North American architect with pretensions tries only to be West Milanese. He has lost sight of his locale. He wants to be international. The architect of the month dominating the international glossy is so busy being world famous he leaves no time for architecture. One month he is the centrefold, then he is forgotten, replaced by yet another. Ephemeral trends take over, revolve and disappear. Urban spaces have become lucky dips for spurious trivialities.

If the architect does withstand the siren calls of showy trends he must still find extra strength. Administrative trivia is loaded onto his shoulders. The modern architectural process is a labyrinth of spurious measures, trivial make-work procedures, flank-protecting legal nonsense to deflect responsibility. The institutional client, feigning concern for the public, has devised a multitude of enervating mind traps to diffuse responsibilities, protecting petty bureaucracies. Architecture is conducted in an imposed atmosphere of fear and legal buck passing. Every one is afraid of the idea, of risk and creativity. Institutionalized safeguards guarantee failure and chaos. The vision is lost in an overwhelming torrent of petty business. After almost two decades of mind numbing, inconsequential discussions on the merits of what are essentially individual idiosyncrasies, architecture gasps for survival. The architect escapes into his own world of jargon, awards and esoteric theorizing.

What has been lost in the current heated debate (while failing incidentally to heat the interested public) is that while *91* great architectural movements were universal they had in common the quality of responding to locality. An international, lasting, historic movement of architecture is identified by the ingenuity applied to the enclosure of space using indigenous materials and habits. An historic movement of architecture is centred in a strong local motivation. Since building began, great architectural styles ran rampant over borders and invaded cultures. But always as a mark of their greatness they shared, across history, one indelible characteristic. As the Romanesque, the Gothic, the baroque movements moved northward into Europe and beyond, so did they adapt to local customs and conditions. While their macrocultural identities remained constant, their details responded to the local mores.

The same cannot be said of modern architecture. For, as modern architecture too crossed borders, it did so in monotonous monolithic form, excepting of course a very few prescient designs. Its allegiance is to the bottom line. Vast, flexible, interior spaces and almost total neglect of public space, other than for spectator convenience, is its mark of spatial architectural motif.

Modern architecture never had adaptability. It is too rigidly doctrinaire. There is no room for adaptation to local conditions. We seem satisfied to import uninterrupted the personal idiosyncrasies of individual architects as given lore because of their "international" reputations. We have lost our consciousness of space or any other identifying marks in relationship to place. We have come to accept the onslaught of the architectural glossy press as our motivation and we express space in lineal tubular emporiums of consumerism; the corridored shopping mall, the strip city street, the get-there-quickly thoroughfare, or the incomprehensibly massive, domed sports/rock assembly cauldrons.

Even the architects at their Saint John conference on urban spaces could find nothing good to say about the current generation of shopping malls. Why then don't they do something about them? Are they, too, in a state of denial?

The banal running apace with the hectic. The architecture of the city veers hectically from the bland to the quixotic. The result is visually painful. Chaos in small doses can be appealing. What we are confronted with in our contemporary city, however, is not so much chaos in tolerable doses but rather an on-going ennui. Contained galaxies of chaos could be exciting and much of it could be manageable. But the city is now an interminable dirge of incessant, shrewd, politically astute, bland block after bland block, interspersed by convoluted, quixotic, health-threatening, sanity-destroying mayhem.

PART II
Long Live Art

5

Downtown Spaces

Of course our cities are in chaos; that's the way we like them. In our own way we have created the ennui and chaos as a mirror image of ourselves. We love the occasional bustle, the competitive pace, the cacophonous din, the opportunity, the risk, the sleaze, glamour, great things happening, new ideas breaking out. We are even addicted to boredom and why not? Who can argue, God knows, who would want to!

Have no doubt there are great moments, despite the consuetudinary mess. In the mayhem there is magnificence. There are occasional places, splendid within the rubble, strung out like a fragile pearl necklace. Some quite resplendent spaces are waiting to be found.

So part II is devoted to illuminating the better side of what we are, to describing some of those pearls. Accordingly, six downtown urban gathering places are described and illustrated to show off some of the best. The six have not been chosen for comparative analysis. Indeed, each stands on its merit. In the absence of a normative they do, however, provide a means for visualizing a baseline of urban proportions and other characteristics in a field of design that is very subjective.

No doubt there are other spaces across the country worthy to be illustrated, but at least five of these six are exemplary. In any case many more than the six are illustrated throughout the book demonstrating other points. These others, in their own way, are just as beautiful. But the six here are dissected to demonstrate the points made in part I as they apply to real circumstances. I hope these places come on as well in drawing as they do in fact for the Canadian city has some urban wonder, although it is sparse and hard to find.

Dissecting urban spaces cannot be a scientific exercise in pedantic comparisons. Comparisons are irrelevant, like comparing apples and oranges. Neither is the intent to be judgemental. One of the great delusions of the twentieth century is that architecture and urban planning are sciences related to technology. How can we make scientific evaluations and comparisons of subjective, often fortuitous, emotionally charged urban spaces between buildings? The architectural and planning professions have been labouring for decades on the assumption their work is a science. And indeed some of it is. By far the greater part is, nevertheless, very subjective, political and elusive.

The city is an agglomeration of contrary habits, scientific folklore to the contrary. The urban spaces illustrated in this chapter have evolved out of shared foresight, civic mistakes, happenstance, incisive planning and whatever other contradictions come to mind. The more we study them, the more they elude description. The city is an elusive condition where people meet for reasons unbeknown even to themselves.

One thing these spaces do have in common: all six are held in great affection. All are special. Dissecting them cannot show what makes these places so affectionately regarded by those who live and work around them. Still, some comments are appropriate.

The spaces are held in particular regard by the community. Some because they are familiar, or because they have been there so long, they are habitual. One or two are there by accident. At least one is there by the good grace and vigilant foresight of a few people with vision. In any event all are now icons of the civic shared vision of their respective urban spaces.

The surrounding architecture is for the most part unspectacular. The spaces are beautiful and unpretentious. Unpretentiousness is their great quality. Their attributes are commonplace and everyday. The buildings come together to make the spaces—some modest, some imposing, some of civic importance but all relating together to make the space complete. Indeed some of the surrounding buildings are invidious hulks evoking questions of why they are there. No matter, they all make their contribution. How they came together is not significant, that they have is.

And those attributes conspire to accumulate the elements of urban space into spaces of great civic affection.

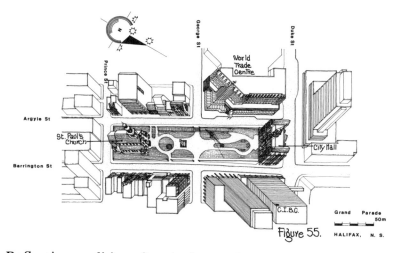

Figure 55.   HALIFAX, N. S.

Reflective qualities of enclosing surfaces, textures, chiaroscuro, angle to the sun of building surfaces directing the sunlight into microclimates all make their contribution. Such are the attributes for which the six have been selected.

The six are: in Halifax, Grand Parade; in Montreal, place d'Armes; in Toronto, Nathan Phillips Square; in Edmonton, Rice-Howard Way; in Vancouver, the Court House Square; and Fan Tan Alley in Victoria.

Grand Parade downtown in Halifax and the significance the space holds in the pattern of streets is shown in figure **46.** Grand Parade, **55,** reflects the fortuitous long block layout of the downtown. Illustration **56** is the footprint of the ground

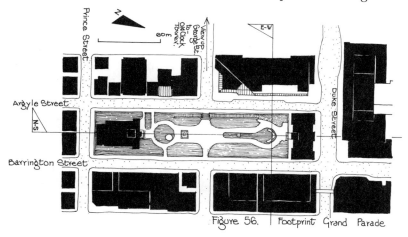

Figure 56.   Footprint Grand Parade

plan describing the building enclosures and the relationships surrounding the space. Busy streets surround Grand Parade, yet it is quiet by general standards, appendices I & II.

Grand Parade, **55,** is an urban park boxed in by Prince, Argyle, Duke and Barrington Streets. In the middle, stands the requisite flag pole with the civic war memorial in the central area. St. Paul's Anglican Church backs onto Prince Street; City Hall opposite backs onto Duke Street. Other surrounding buildings in **56,** the footprint plan, are The World Trade and Convention Centre on Argyle between George and Duke, Duke Tower office building behind City Hall and the Bank of Commerce and the TD Bank towers on Barrington between George and Duke.

98

Two buildings declare the space, St. Paul's Church and City Hall. They stand gently regarding one another, obviously old pals. A third building shares a presence on the space although it is sited well away, the Old Town Clock. Its presence closes the vista up George Street to the Citadel. The Clock Tower is impossible to ignore, it stands so high on the rising hill of George Street.

These three treasured pieces are as modest as they are impressive. Their presence commands the space in the face of looming modern structures that compete for their attention. St. Paul's, the oldest Protestant church in Canada, is not unusual so far as painted clapboard churches go. White painted wooden siding, green painted trim, restoration spire gesture a church facade. But its siting facing the brownstone City Hall makes the space unique, unusual. Grand Parade has an ambience all its own.

The City Hall, built about 150 years after the church, is obviously reciprocating the general proportions of the church spire in its own central pinnacle. Both are approximately the same height, being 0.4 and 0.3, section **57,** and, **58,** of the length between. So at each end of the space there is a rhyme of formal composition. Quite a design. Was it intentional?

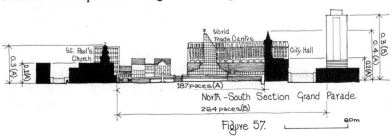

Figure 57.

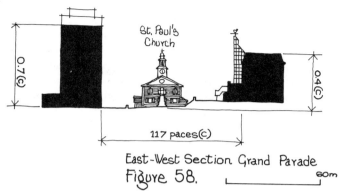

St. Paul's
Church

0.7(C)

0.4(C)

117 paces(C)

East-West Section Grand Parade
Figure 58.

80m

An explanation of the section illustrations should be inserted before continuing. And the following explanation applies to all the section illustrations in the book. Horizontal measurements are described as paces and that is always denoted as dimension (A), (B) or (C). One pace is 0.75 of one metre. Buildings in section are shown as black masses. Their heights are described as a proportion of the horizontal dimension (A) or (B). Thus the heights of the buildings shown in 57 are, for instance, 0.2(A), 0.3(A) and 0.4(A), a percentage of dimension (A) which is 187 paces. Building height 0.3 of 187 paces (the dimension A) is 56 paces, or 42 metres and so on.

But City Hall and the church are not the only buildings that make the place. The World Trade and Convention Centre, designed by Dumaresq and Byrne in 1985, makes a contribution. Built in the 1980s its presence is unusual, given the propensity of modern architecture to intrude. Faced by textured masonry, warm colours, and a smooth reflecting glass pinnacle, nautically topped, the Convention Centre gives to the space in a manner not often attributable to a modern building. Fortunately, the surrounding modern tower office buildings are set away from the main surface of Grand Parade itself, across the streets and behind the trees and are thus obscure.

There is no suggested magic in the proportions and numbers. However, height compared to ground level scantlings does help us to understand propinquity in the relationship of building surfaces. The unimposing scale of the space is attributable to these proportions. The two main buildings that set the general character follow a scale appropriate for their time, long before office towers could be engineered. Nevertheless, this is not a grand space despite the name, and indeed that is its charm. But the proportions are eminently in keeping with the courteous nature of the city. Obviously, Grand Parade demonstrates this through its low key ambience.

Furthermore, the spatial impression is confirmed by those proportions. Grand Parade space is in the form of a dish. Unlike the dish form of Olympic Plaza, Calgary, Grand Parade is smaller and exudes an urban ambience. The spatial lines of influence, **59,** are not intense. And their weak flow from the centre of the plaza draws the observer's attention to the distant skyline towers. Sited behind the predominant buildings, the church and City Hall, the office towers are a subdued looming presence making the skyline less imminent. And the textures of the lower scale buildings orchestrate, with those buildings on and around the parade very well.

100

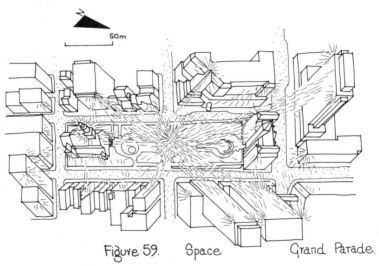

50m

Figure 59. &pace Grand Parade.

Dish-like, Grand Parade is good for sun exposure. Fortuitous orientations ensure almost continuous sunshine on the space during usable hours. The shape, **60,** is long, narrow and sloping: Halifax downtown streets follow the contours. The shadows shown in the illustration are noon, mid-summer. But for the trees this could be oppressive. In winter, on the other hand, the shadows are not so long that the space is ever in the bleak shade. The textured colouring of the building fronts temper the light, reflecting back a warm glow. Most of the surfaces get the sun some time.

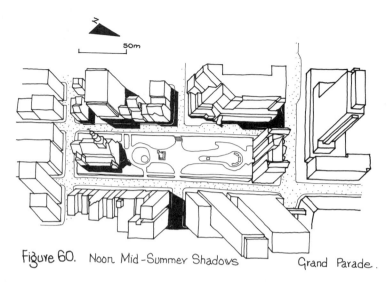

Figure 60. Noon Mid-Summer Shadows   Grand Parade.

Swarming between the warm-textured building surfaces and the reposing centre of the park is the traffic. Grand Parade is boxed in by the traffic. Spaces that were built in slower times always suffer this isolation, becoming traffic islands. Grand Parade is no exception, although its accumulated attributes temper the more disturbing intrusion and the noise. Traffic intensity is represented, **61,** by the boldness of the directional arrows. The heavier the arrow the more intense the traffic. The dotted lines represent pedestrian movement.

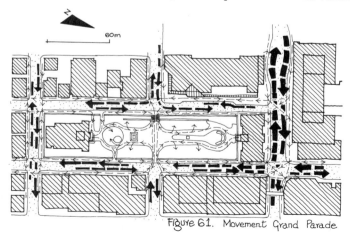

Figure 61. Movement Grand Parade

Park traffic is not exclusive to pedestrians. A few vehicles are allowed and parking is provided. But the central park surface is the domain of the walking, listening (for concerts are performed in summer), girl watching, boy watching, lunch eating public. Popular it is too. The public uses it in droves. The spatial enclosure is complete, **62.** The propinquity of City Hall seen in the same view as the well-sited and beautifully composed Convention Centre, with St. Paul's is something to behold. Even the office towers, incidentally relegated to the background by the dish-like configuration, are less prominent than the trees and the flag pole in the central span of vision. Grand Parade is one significant Canadian urban space.

So is place d'Armes a significant Canadian public urban space. Place d'Armes is one of our few truly urban spaces in Canada: truly urban in Robert Allsopp's sense. Centrally situated in the Old City of Montreal, **1,** the place has all the attributes listed above in "The Elements of Urban Space". In fact in my opinion it is the most magnificent public urban space north of the Rio Grande.

When Montreal was the financial centre of Canada, clearly place d'Armes was the financial centre of Montreal. Appropriately the surrounding buildings are banks and a church. Today it exudes the luxury of a well spent past.

Place d'Armes, **63,** could not be mistaken for an urban park, not according to Allsopp. It is an urban place. The locus of converging lines of movement of important streets describe the space. Four of these streets converge naturally at

Figure 62. Grand Parade Halifax

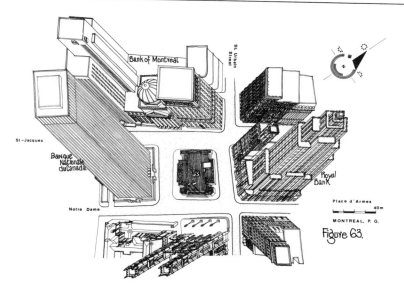

St. Urbain Street

St-Jacques

Banque Nationale du Canada

Bank of Montreal

Royal Bank

Notre Dame

Place d'Armes
40m
MONTREAL, P. Q.

Figure 63.

the central place. The street surfaces form an integral part of the space. Saint-Jacques, St. Urbain, Saint-Sulpice and Notre Dame streets converge here and move again into the street fabric as a part of the Old City.

The surrounding buildings, **63,** are: starting with the modern tower on the south-west side, la Banque Nationale du Canada; on the north-west face are the Bank of Montreal buildings spreading from Saint-Urbain to Saint-François-Xavier; the north-east face is occupied by the old Quebec Bank and the art deco tower of the Royal Bank of Canada; Notre Dame Church, the presbytery and le Vieux Séminaire complete the space on the south-east face. The columnated, domed building on the north-west face is the grand banking hall of the Bank of Montreal.

Unlike so many public urban spaces, place d'Armes is described, aligned, characterized and depicted by its surrounding buildings. The early stages of development were characterized by an accretion process. Commencing in 1684 with the seminary, there was an acknowledged understanding that the building surfaces must contribute to the sense of space by aligning with the surfaces of the space. As the Sherbrooke Wall defines the street alignment of Sherbrooke Street, so do the building surfaces define place d'Armes. In the days of its inception there was an implicit understanding, a vision shared amongst the separate developers, to build to

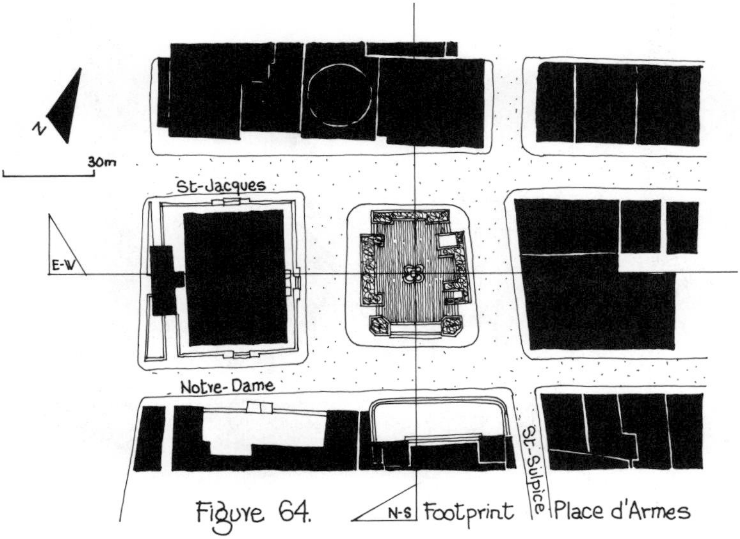

Figure 64. N-S Footprint Place d'Armes

the street line surrounding the space. The footprint plan, **64,** demonstrates this. In those days there was no need for urban design guide-lines.

The process of accretion occurred in three major phases. The building of the space was carried out over many generations. The shared vision was handed down intact until the present era. During the middle years of the nineteenth century place d'Armes flourished. The subsequent phases of building activity continued into the 1930s and the present era.

The 1960s tower is the contribution of the present era. The tower of the *la Banque Nationale du Canada* is an anomaly. Out of place in the place d'Armes context it is just another listless piece of commercial modernism. Yet, the inherent architectural ugliness of the tower is so diffuse and weak as not to detract from the beauty of its setting. The quality of its surroundings ensures its place. The tower cannot be assessed standing alone. The surrounding buildings and their relationships give the space its life. If one lacks architectural strength, it is carried by the rest. The design qualities of each building in this space gives credibility to the contention that design of individual buildings can be enhanced by the relationships of the whole.

Place d'Armes is a composite of textured surfaces and smoothness, of old and new. There is a gradation of permeability on all the surfaces. The least absorbing surface is

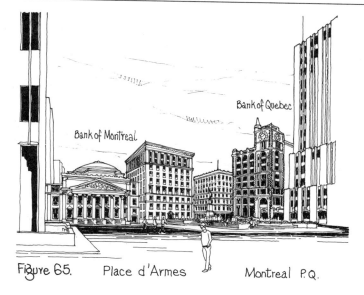

Figure 65.   Place d'Armes   Montreal P.Q.

105

la Banque Nationale, the most absorbing is the portico and pediment of the Bank of Montreal banking hall. Together they complement one another.

The buildings rhyme a vertical motif, **65.** More or less, the facades reflect a metre of verticals, pilasters, windows, columns and steeples. The proportions of the buildings are upright and their close proximity accentuate a vertical ambience.

The cross sections, **66** and **67,** show height variations in the cross sections of place d'Armes from very low, 0.3 proportion of building height to the north/south width, to 1.4 proportion of building height to the east/west width. The

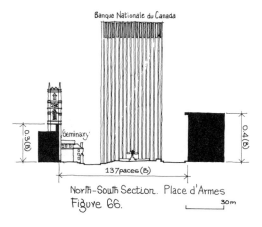

North-South Section. Place d'Armes
Figure 66.   30m

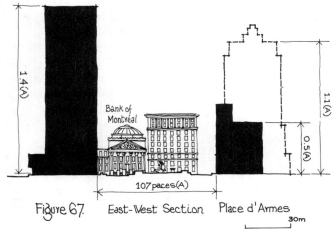

Bank of
Montréal

1.4(A)

1.1(A)

0.5(A)

107 paces(A)

Figure 67.   East-West Section   Place d'Armes

30m

sections show how the tower actually adds to the ambience of the space; it sets up wide contrasts in height, as well as contrasts in other elements. And the contrast is within a scale that is not beyond a pedestrian's reach. If the tower were alone it would show few redeeming features. But it is not alone, it is a part of the composition of place d'Armes. Contrast of the heights and the widths, contrast of the smooth modern surfaces with the textured heritage surfaces, contrast of the chiaroscuro of the banking hall's columned portico with the

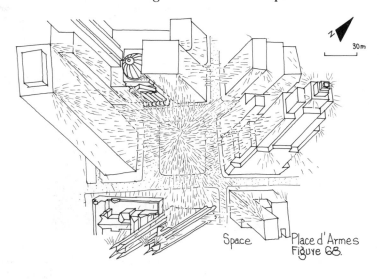

N

30m

Space   Place d'Armes
Figure 68.

lack of it on the tower. All of the contrasts are inherent in the surfaces and the building forms; nothing is extraneous to the ambience.

Contrast is not all. This is a small space but it is a composite that has accumulated a lot of interesting architectural qualities. Not the least of which is the intense spatial relationships set up between the building facades, **68**. Propinquity plays a large part in this spatial intensity. The smooth surface seems to draw out and accentuate the texture of the older buildings and the lines of influence zing between them.

The brisk spatial interaction is accentuated by light play. In summer place d'Armes is full of people, not only tourists but working people from the surrounding offices. The central pedestrian surface inside the traffic circulation surfaces is full *107* of activity. This is the place where sunshine has its greatest effect. Not surprisingly, because of the tower, this area is also most often in the shade, **69**. Is this a disadvantage? For the casual tourist, no, it is not. In the heat of Montreal's midday summer sun, shade can be a blessing. In the morning the space is bathed in bright sunshine. In the late afternoon the shade has gone. At midday when the sun is most intense the shade is in the right place, on the central pedestrian space. Only in the spring and fall, are the shadows of the tower least effective.

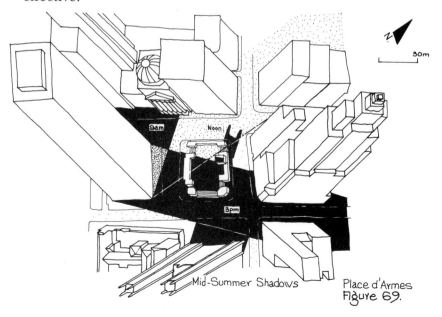

Mid-Summer Shadows

Place d'Armes
Figure 69.

Winter brings another face. For then place d'Armes is peaceful. No one is around; it is deserted. The central pedestrian space is covered with snow to half a metre, with not so much as a footprint to show that someone has been there. Shadows do not matter then. Winter is best, for there is no one there; no buses, no lost driving tourists, just a glistening quiet.

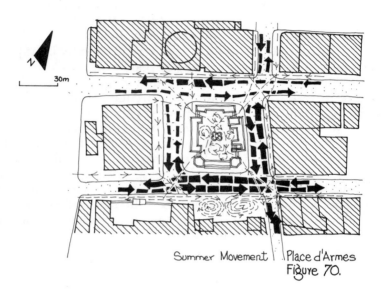

Summer Movement   Place d'Armes
Figure 70.

Street traffic, **70,** is congested, just the way we like it. But the grain is uneven, out of balance with the buses, for place d'Armes is a magnet for tourists. They come and go in buses that park before the church. And in the summer heat the buses need their air conditioning and keep their motors running. Yes, the incessant, growling whine of buses persists all day long, all summer long. The noise is unbelievable, look at the appendices, they're way above tolerances. With the whine comes haze, an invidious reeking diesel, blue, lingering out of focus, playing havoc with the microclimate.

Tourists are so much a part of city life, it is hard to imagine that once this space was the centre of a national image, the power of finance and the power of the church. Well, this shows on the skyline, **71,** of the Old Port. Church pinnacles, bank towers thrusting upwards that once dominated the country now just dominate the skyline.

Banque Nationale
du Canada.

Royal
Bank

109

Figure 71.

Place d'Armes from the port.

Power moved to Toronto. Not the power of the church, the power of finance. And how well Nathan Phillips Square, **72,** depicts that sense of power. The square started Toronto on its way to being a great world city.

Nathan Phillips Square as medium represents Toronto. The new Toronto City Hall, **73,** dominates. Viljo Revell

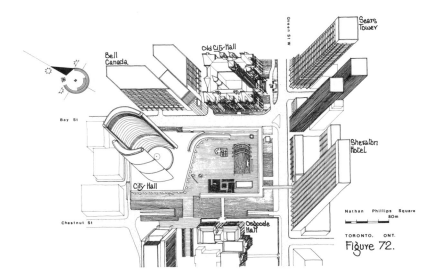

Sears
Tower

Old City Hall

Bell
Canada

Queen St W

Bay St

Sheraton
Hotel

City Hall

Chestnut St

Osgoode
Hall

Nathan   Phillips   Square
80m

TORONTO.   ONT.

Figure 72.

Figure 73. ———————— New City Hall, Toronto.

designed two clasping towers to be the vertical emblem on the north side. It was completed in 1965 after a very well publicized international architectural competition. On Bay Street directly across to the east are the offices of Bell Canada. Next to it, still on Bay street, on the corner of Queen Street West is the old City Hall. Old City hall, designed by E. J. Lennox, was completed sixty-seven years before the new one.

Little did the architect visualize, then, how important his Romanesque design would be as a foil to the severe modernism that later took over. To the south across Queen Street West is the Sheraton Centre, concrete towers enclosing the south skyline. And Osgoode Hall, the low classical building, is to the west behind the trees.

The cliff side of buildings surrounding Nathan Phillips is not an inter-relationship of buildings. It is rather a spatial sum of each building standing separately. The clasping form of the new City Hall wraps around rationing space in small doses. Then, as if gratuitously, spills it out for everyone to see. The architecture is massive chiaroscuro. It clings to light, shade and space selfishly, denying it north of the city, turning its back. The space is literally dominated by vast towers. Yet, the scale and ambience is set up by the girdling modest elevated walkway, defending the open surface from the hassle of the streets.

The vast and dominating towers are no match for the attention-attracting details of the older buildings, the old City Hall and Osgoode Hall. For the old City Hall is one of the great classical buildings of the city. It shows how important the preservation of heritage architecture is in these endless concrete spasms of reinvented urban space. The old Registry Office went without a whimper. It was demolished years ago, fortuitously, to be replaced by the new City hall. Had Lennox's building gone the same way, interaction of the ensuing space would have been non-existent, truly flat. To think that at one time a fight had to be put up to save it seems incredible; it came close to being replaced by the Eaton's Centre. Yet, that is the beauty and strength of Toronto.

The square is an amalgam of high art and disarray. Anything goes from hot dogs to Henry Moore. What a fight they had to get that combination. Fight it was to get Henry Moore on the square and the fight gives a good idea of how Toronto's shared vision of urban space came about. When in 1966 Philip Givens, then the mayor, seized the Moore opportunity he was very nearly reviled. Now over twenty years later anyone who tried to remove it would be reviled. The shared vision had to be pushed. They had to push for the new City Hall, they had to push to save the old one. Now, no one would

111

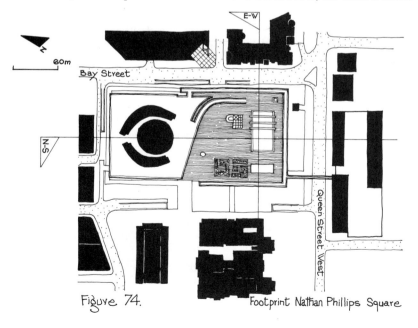

Figure 74.   Footprint Nathan Phillips Square

have it any other way. The shared vision was pushed into being, so the sidewalk supervisors could say, "I told you so".

The footprint, **74,** shows the relationship of the towering buildings, how their positions profile the outer skyline of the square. The surrounding elevated sky walk compresses the square into a closed meeting with the new City Hall. It accentuates the feeling of the space unifying what could have been chaos at the base line: differing building fronts on the streets and cumbersome parking ports.

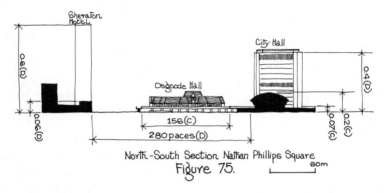

North-South Section Nathan Phillips Square
Figure 75.

Sections, north-south, **75,** and east-west, **76,** show that although the surrounding towers are quite high, proportions of the space are modest. There is no dominating theme of vertical versus horizontal. And if it were not for the enclosing sky walk there would be no cohesive visual form to keep it all together. In fact, the sky walk is Revell's major mark of genius.

Vertical / horizontal tension is not present in the architectural composition and the ambience is languid. Architecture emphasizes vertical form at the expense of horizontal variation. Inter-activity of lines of influence between buildings

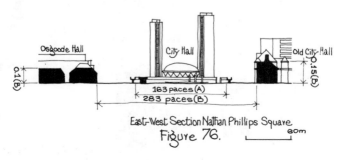

East-West Section Nathan Phillips Square
Figure 76.

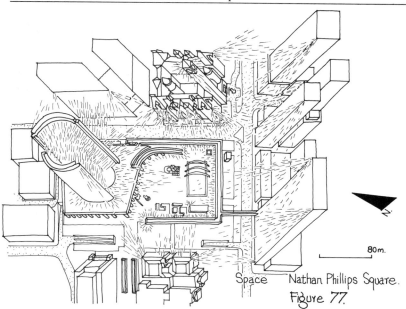

113

Space Nathan Phillips Square.
Figure 77.

is not animated. Proportions are too massive to excite interplay of architectural form. Accordingly, Nathan Phillips
Square is not an urban space in the true sense but more an
urban park. The whole space exists quite independent of the
surrounding city and, figure **77** shows clearly the feeling.

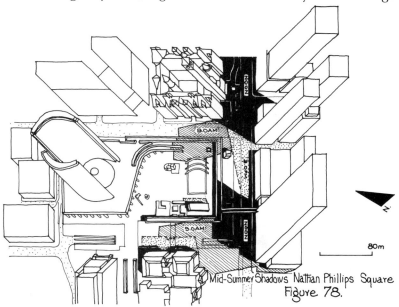

Mid-Summer Shadows Nathan Phillips Square
Figure 78.

Massive buildings cast shadows on Nathan Phillips Square. Often on the wrong spots. Summer time when the shade is needed, **78,** the shadow of the highest tower does not shade the square at noon. The ubiquitous bright concrete of the plaza surface reflects hard light making an overcast summer sky too hard to bear, hot and oppressive.

In winter, **79,** shadows unpleasantly block sun from the skating pond. The largest tower casts its shadow in the very place it isn't wanted. Someone should move that tower. At noon, right on the spot where skaters enjoy the winter noon break, most of the winter sun is gone. Too late now, we are not playing with dominoes.

Movement of busy traffic, **80,** doesn't affect pedestrians strolling on the plaza. Surrounding traffic hardly affects activities on the main plaza surface at all. The elevated walkway successfully isolates the activities from distracting traffic on surrounding streets.

Stand in the middle of Nathan Phillips Square and read the medium of its presence for it is a microcosm of the city, a nut shell idea of what Toronto stands for. General ambience on the square is dense, confusing, interesting, energetic, commanding and littered. The implicit metaphor is Toronto

114

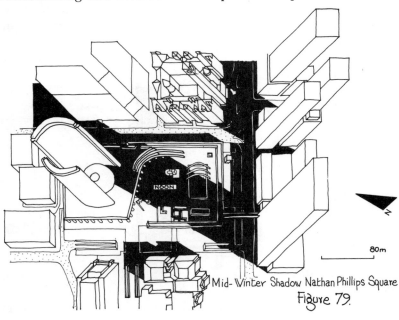

80m

Mid-Winter Shadow Nathan Phillips Square
Figure 79.

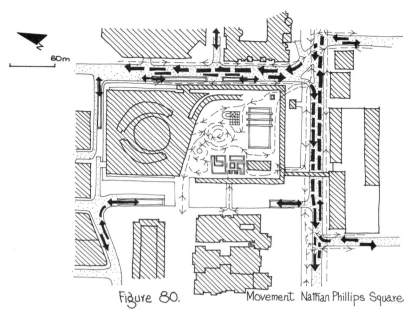

Figure 80.   Movement Nathan Phillips Square

115

girdled. The surface of the square is tightly reigned in by the elevated walkway bodice girdling the remaining pretensions of Toronto's worldly dominance. Inside the girdle Toronto plays. Little things: the peace park, a hot dog stand and *The Archer* litter the surface. Freedom stops outside, at the elevated walkway, the girdle. Behave, it says, no playing outside the girdle of pretensions. Outside, the traffic snarls.

Rice-Howard Way, **81,** evokes a magnificence message of a different sort. This is an interconnecting pedestrian way wending its way amidst a forest of imposing buildings. So imposing, the pedestrian may feel overwhelmed. Indeed, Rice-Howard Way could contribute more to downtown Edmonton if, instead of overwhelming, it attracted people.

Downtown Edmonton shares conditions common to many cities. Too many suburban attractions, too many retail outlets pursuing too few customers, a simplistic quick fix approach and a downtown withering magnificently. Rice-Howard is no West Edmonton Mall. Although with the effort and energy already invested into the pedestrian system of which Rice-Howard is a part it can hardly be called a quick fix. Nevertheless, it was initiated to counteract the incredibly strong drawing power of West Edmonton Mall which is taking people away from the downtown.

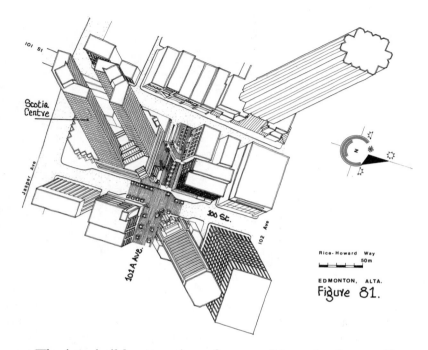

101 St

Scotia
Centre

Jasper Ave

100 St.

102 Ave

101A Ave

Rice-Howard Way
50 m

EDMONTON, ALTA.
Figure 81.

The irresistible attraction of many of the suburban malls, especially the West Edmonton Mall, is a lesson in the powerful use of visual stimuli and persuasive sensory incentives that designers use to seduce customers. Have no doubt, West Edmonton Mall is well designed. The spatial ambience of the interior streets and plazas is a potent lesson for urban designers and planners. Whatever secrets of urban design there are, it has been common knowledge in the advertising industry for years. Architects and planners who have studied work done at the Chicago Institute of Design, Moholy-Nagy and Kepes, during the 40s will be acquainted with the persuasive techniques. To use the same techniques in urban design now would not be trite. And Rice-Howard Way could use them.

Rice-Howard Way is a part of a pedestrian system that networks across downtown Edmonton, 82. Jasper Avenue, Rice-Howard Way, Chinatown and the Heritage Trail are an integrated system known locally as PRIDE, the acronym for Program to Improve Downtown Edmonton. The PRIDE program ostensibly elevates the image of downtown into a recognized winter city and a viable alternative to the suburban shopping malls. Success of the program is moot!

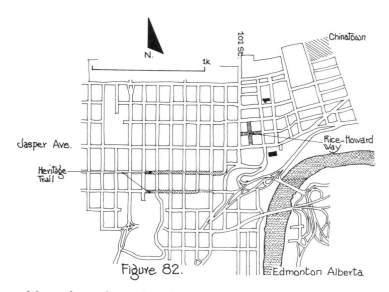

Figure 82.

More than glossy handouts will be needed to do that, for the program makes no recommendations of drastic architectural measures. PRIDE turns out to be a diluted beautification attempt only the most trenchant booster would support. The dominant grid layout and traffic circulation of the street pattern remains unchallenged. There is little to show that any real spatial activity, what could be described as more than conventional street activity, has been generated. The centres, Rice-Howard Way, Chinatown etc., are so sparsely located, the impact of their presence is hardly noticed. As is so often the case, promotional literature like PRIDE handouts give temporary highs to city hall officials but little else.

The footprint plan of Rice-Howard Way, **83,** shows the intersection of 101A Avenue and 100 Street. The enclosing buildings are in the following order. On the north-west corner is a canopied four-storey heritage facade replete with restaurants. The Phipps, McKinnon office tower is on the northeast corner. Across on the south-east corner is a parking garage and the Scotia Bank tower takes up the south side of the south-west corner.

The alignment of the street, that is, the wall of facades enclosing the space, has been maintained except for the angled siting of the Phipps, McKinnon tower. And this angled siting is obtrusive and spatial effect is undramatic. New building facades would have been more effective had they been consistently designed to respect a pedestrian quality and activity at street level. None of the elements of architectural urban space have been followed; indeed, the design appears to have neglected ambience in favour of design expediency. Surface treatment that attracts the eye, compatibility of textures, chiaroscuro, does not exist.

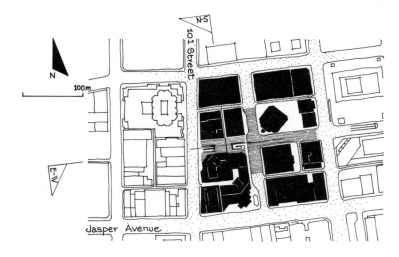

Figure 83. Footprint Rice-Howard Way

Plastique is happenstance. Propinquity has been left to habitual placing rather than considered relationships. The spaces between the buildings come out of the two-dimensional street patterns, no modification, no manipulation of space. Unfortunately for pedestrian activity, the original

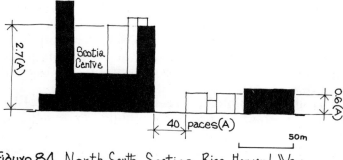

Figure 84. North-South Section Rice-Howard Way

street pattern was drafted on a map with no consideration for either a mix of traffic or separation, back to the castrum again. The shared vision of urban space is still the conventional block layout of the engineering draftsmen. The legal lot lines were followed; the buildings were plunked on their respective sites; the separateness of the buildings is extenuated and the continuity of space is ignored.

Section drawings, **84** and **85,** of the intersection show the buildings are quite different in heights and architectural forms, some excessively high, some conventionally low. The Scotia Bank tower has an overwhelming and looming presence 2.7 times taller than the width of the pedestrian space it encloses. The scale of the tower is incomprehensible. It cannot be seen from the level of the pedestrian way. Only by walking away down 101 Street may the observer grasp the vertical form as it dominates the space. And on the other side of Rice-Howard Way the heritage buildings are 0.6 of the pedestrian way. Can the heritage buildings hold their own? Hardly.

119

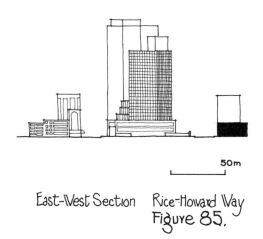

East-West Section   Rice-Howard Way
Figure 85.

Spatially, **86,** the lines of influence interacting between the buildings are not exciting. Interrelationships are little different from any other street in the downtown core. The directional, relentless, one-dimensional, lineal traffic street form is unabated. Light, shade and sunshine, **87,** bounce off the harsh, reflective surfaces of the buildings in a manner that makes it difficult to relax and enjoy what should be a reposeful atmosphere to enhance the cafés. Light quality is harsh.

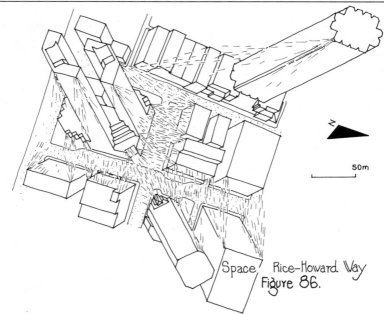

Space / Rice-Howard Way
Figure 86.

120

This part of the Rice-Howard Way pedestrian system is one short block, just below the Scotia Bank tower, **88.** There are no architectural features to identify it from traffic streets. Clay paving ubiquitous throughout the downtown is used

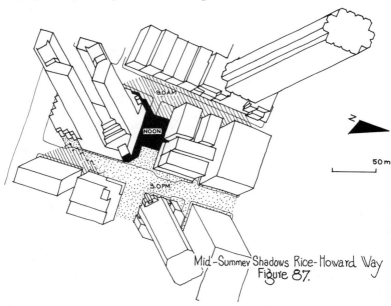

Mid-Summer Shadows Rice-Howard Way
Figure 87.

here. What impact it could have is lost through so much use. Red paving covers flat pavements without direction, relief or discernible purpose.

Motion on the Way is the street traffic expected of any normal street. Only one small block has been reserved for pedestrians, of that a good third is entrance to underground parking.

As for ritual, there are some café tables on the pedestrian surface, but the general surface activity is cars parked, cars moving and pedestrians watching out. The design intent of Rice-Howard Way is weak. It has little effect in view of the demanding presence of the large towers and intense traffic.

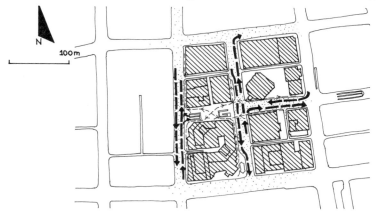

121

Figure 88.   Movement Rice-Howard Way

Evident on the Rice-Howard pedestrian way is a lack of grace that demonstrates the difficulties presented when a city has been built on the rectangular block layout without consideration for spatial pauses: the military or railway engineer's dream of the West. West Edmonton Mall is a very compelling draw away from downtown Edmonton. Clearly it will continue so until something creatively drastic is done to counter its powerful attraction. Art, after all, is risk and until city design is elevated to an art form merchants downtown will continue to feel the monetary privation that comes from trusting in the short-term balance sheet rather than their shared vision of the city. If once the city is laid out in the configuration of rectilinear traffic patterns it is very difficult to retrieve it for the pedestrian.

Fortunately, this did not happen in Vancouver. The ec-
centricities of the block layout aside, Vancouver's streets have
retained an element of interest for the pedestrian by simply
leaving open space on the rectangular blocks. As there are
only four—Sky Train Park, Oceanic Park, Victory Square and
Court House Square in the downtown—the accumulated impact is quite effective.

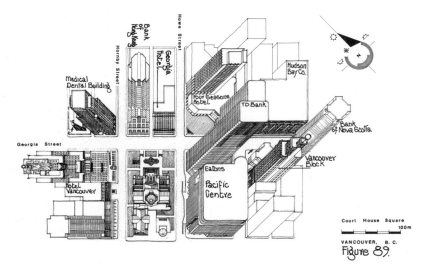

Court House Square

VANCOUVER, B. C.

Figure 89.

Court House Square, **89,** another example of a good urban space, is an open space in front of the old court house,
now the Art Gallery. Spatially it forms the northern part of the
system of open space and public enclosure known as the Robson Complex. Within this complex is the New Court House,
the Robson Media Centre, the Vancouver Art Gallery and the
Court House Square. People mistake the space for an entrance garden to the Art Gallery. The main entrance steps to
what used to be the Court House spring from the surface
there. Still the central focus of the city now seems to have
grown up around it. Court House Square is indeed an icon for
the city.

The icon of the urban space has survived as an integral
piece in the urban jigsaw of Vancouver for over seventy years.
Following the footprint plan, **90,** the buildings surrounding
the square are, starting on the north corner of Georgia and
Hornby, the Georgia Medical Dental Building, which will,
when this book is published, miraculously emerge from its

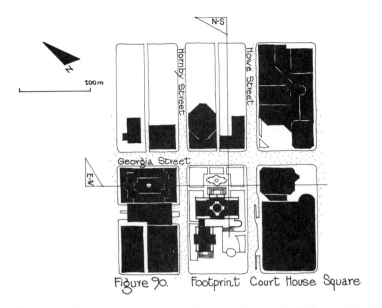

Figure 90.   Footprint Court House Square

traditional chrysalis as the Cathedral Plaza Building, **31.** Following eastward along Georgia is the Bank of Hong Kong Building, the Georgia Hotel and the Pacific Centre Plaza. Across Georgia on the south side is the Court House Square with the Vancouver Art Gallery set back from the street front which, indeed, is the reason for the square. On the east of

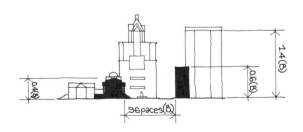

North-South Section Court House Square
Figure 91.

the Square is the Eaton's Centre and the Vancouver Hotel is to the west.

The sections, **91, 92,** show an urban space with a reasonably balanced set of vertical proportions. The TD Bank tower is not out of alignment with the Vancouver Hotel and the Georgia Hotel seems to be set down appropriately with the Art Gallery across the square. The surrounding effect of the buildings is that they follow the spatial alignment on the streets, their height is not overwhelming and the proportions of the buildings suit one another. There is a neighbourliness about the interrelationship of the buildings, despite their congruent disparity. The modern intruding buildings tend to depend for their architectural quality upon being neighbours with the traditional buildings. The fact that most of the enclosing surfaces are textured, and following the light and shadow play of chiaroscuro obscures the license taken in the modern designs to ignore good urban design principles.

124

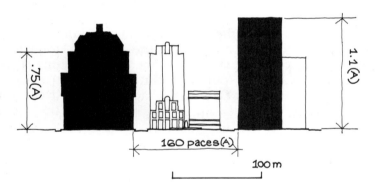

East-West Section Court House Square
Figure 92.

Plastique, the architectural form of Court House Square, is an urban rectangular block. Surrounding buildings line up with the streets. Facade alignment of all the buildings has been respected. Facades complement the civic significance and the sense of place. Vistas have been framed to show off the waterfront looking down Hornby and Howe Streets. A distinct urban ambience prevails by virtue of the accumulated effects of the architectural attributes of each building as it relates to its neighbour.

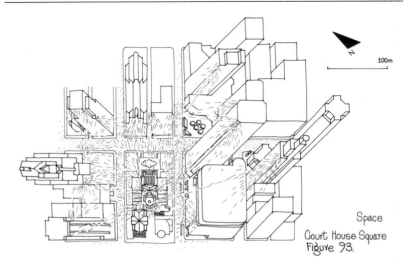

Space

Court House Square

Figure 93.

125

Separateness of building designs seems to be mitigated by the relatively small scale. There has been no intended interrelationship in the design of the buildings, but fortuitously, relationships are there. The stark design of the modern structures is no less imposing than in any other contemporary urban space, but fortunately, the scale of the total space brings all their disparate forms together.

Propinquity of the buildings is separate enough as to militate against an intensely vibrant interrelationship between building facades. Spatially, in **93,** the ambience is diluted, although not unpleasantly so. The buildings to the south do not predominate, so sun comes beaming in to play spatially with ground surface patterns. Shadows, **94,** do come to the Art Gallery steps for most of the day. Those steps are where people like to sit most of the warmer days. However, it is the south side of the Art Gallery that is populated with people watchers and that is where the main entrance is and all people activities are generated.

Court House Square is busy and noisy. Much of the noise comes from regular city traffic. The decibel level (appendices I & II), is too high for a reposeful urban space. Less noise and sun are why people congregate on the south side. But lunch time people watchers, well inured to city noise by now, do lie out on the lawn in the isolated centre of the space. Evidently some people can relax anywhere.

The central space, isolated by traffic, is becoming a repetitive urban condition throughout all modern cities. It is the

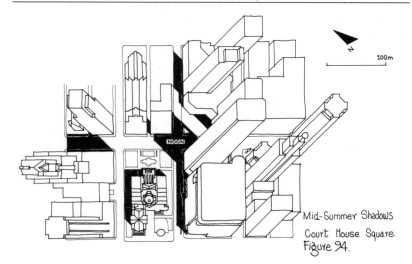

Mid-Summer Shadows
Court House Square
Figure 94.

outcome of the rectangular circulation patterns. We have been compelled to rationalize quality and ambience, ignoring as best we can the noise factor. This is a general condition in the twentieth century city. It is not unique to Court House Square. Circulation, **95,** shows very busy streets, the source of the noise, surrounding the three open sides of the square. Noise is amplified by the box shape of the enclosure. Resonance is amplified by the hard smooth surfaces. The square is an integral part of the city circulation and spatial patterns, but it comes at a high price of spatial repose and quiet.

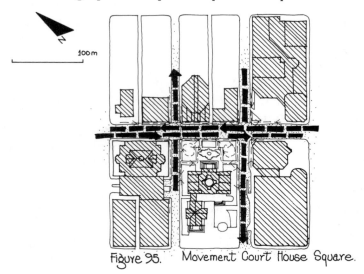

Figure 95.   Movement Court House Square.

Spatial repose is not at issue in Fan Tan Alley, Victoria, **96.** Fan Tan Alley is an important part of the pedestrian circulation network in the old part of town. A confined urban space, an alley-way, it has not been included here to be facetious. It is a truly viable commercial, going concern. And as a traditional part of the circulation pattern it is an opportunity that could be overlooked in any redeveloping downtown. Fortunately, the alley has been there so long the planners had to bend the rules: outside, exposed fire-prevention sprinklers, for instance, to make it a part of the city. Otherwise, over-enthusiastic modernists could have caused its demise. Fan Tan Alley has been a part of Victoria's Chinatown for as long as that part of the city has been used.

127

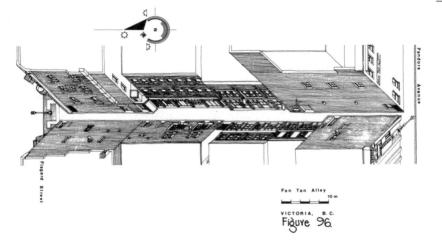

Fan Tan Alley
10 m
VICTORIA, B.C.
Figure 96.

The footprint plan, **97,** of Fan Tan Alley gives the impression of an oversight between parcels of real estate. No one would plan for a space, or a pedestrian walkway like this today. Civic ordinances would prevent it happening. We just don't think this way any more, at least the professionals don't. And more's the pity, for a space such as Fan Tan Alley, flying as it does in the face of what is considered to be proper urban design standard scantlings, is a good example of people using space to its ultimate purpose.

Contrary to convention, this space or pedestrian thoroughfare illustrates how a set of imposed rigid rules can be made flexible to everyone's advantage. The rigid rules are the engineering standards set by most cities to ensure access to

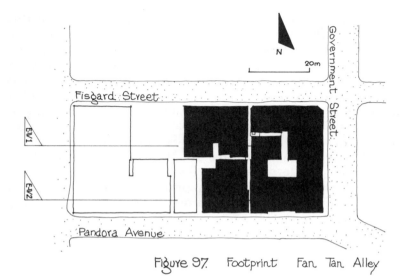

Figure 97.   Footprint   Fan Tan Alley

light, free movement of circulation and the general, but un-
questioned, standard of modern design in use today. Some of
these conventional rules we would be well advised to recon-
sider, if we are serious about re-invigorating the urban environment in a manner that will bring life back, in a manner we
profess to desire. Modern developments could be designed to
a more humane purpose if the scantlings of Fan Tan Alley
were emulated.

   Vertical proportions such as those in Fan Tan Alley
would be horrendous if the scale were larger. Two east-west
sections, **98,** display a looming building presence that would
be untenable if the other compatible architectural qualities

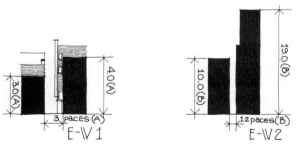

Figure 98.   East–West Sections   Fan Tan Alley

were absent, scale being the most important quality in this circumstance. As it is, the scale is compatible with human use even though the building height may be nineteen times the width of the space. Section E-W2, shows the width is only 1.2 paces wide, hardly sufficient space for two people to pass.

The buildings facing onto the space follow the alignment of the alley out of necessity. Minor variations in the alignment are clearly unintentional but they add measurably to the effectiveness of the space. The facades are textured and rich in warm, coloured masonry. Windows and doorways open from small stores, offices and a woodworking shop. Activity is intensified by the confining nature of the space. And the spatial lines of influence, **99,** are proportionately intensified by the close proximity of the enclosing faces.

129

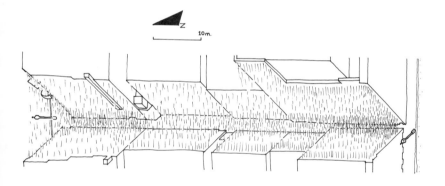

Figure 99. Space. Fan Tan Alley

Fan Tan Alley has been included to demonstrate the unconventional: how to catch the spontaneous opportunities of urban space. In this small casual instance can be found a lesson showing how reality transcends conventional standards. Designs on paper, approved and institutionalized standards, and what works on the street are often worlds apart.

The six urban spaces that have been discussed in this chapter are worlds apart in their form, character and impressions. Comparison has been avoided. They have been illustrated to exemplify the range of possibilities inherent in the design of public urban space, not so much as following a set of defined conventions, but as a way of grasping opportunities while holding to a set of values. If hopes are realized, some of those values may be derived by respecting a collective vision of urban space, translating that shared vision into a way of imagining space, then making it work by combining those architectural characteristics that make a city space worth having.

130

6
Malls and Streets

All spaces between buildings could be transformed into spaces for people if we exercise our imaginations. Lanes, back alleys, service areas, parking stalls and left over space are all worth designing beautifully. We tend not to see most urban space as usable unless it is built up or as chunks of left over land with a bit of grass with perennial borders. Lanes are for garbage trucks! Unwittingly our priorities became defined many years ago. More than good intentions now will turn the situation around.

The early seventies was a time for "the people" to take back the cities. Bulldozers were halted in their tracks; freeways were rolled back; housing was returned to the neighbourhoods. Big bad high-rises were on the descent. Local improvements were completed and "the people" were happy in their kingdom. "Places for people", that was the slogan. Build it for "the people"! And many people places were made.

The outcome of those good intentions can be seen in the malls and streets that were created then and are still regaling the city today. Every city in the country boasts a completed (or in the process of development) mall or people place. Places for the people come in the form of improved streets, beautified by boulevard trees, paving, bicycle racks, mini-parks and lines of shops. Streets have been converted into pedestrian malls, bus malls and transit malls. Some of them come resplendent with farmers' markets and brand new shopping malls. Ethnic neighbourhoods have been defined: Chinatown, Cabbagetown, little Italy. Fabulous, the smells send us swooning. These are the urban hot spots of today.

Not all of them evolved as was expected. Some turned

out well; some of them not quite so well. We envisaged bustling market places, medieval market places, the eastern bazaar and the friendly barter of interchange. Those beautiful artists' interpretations of the malls were treated to beautiful ladies strutting to the fashion shops, happy children playing and happy merchants ringing up their tills. In the excitement of those public meetings when the concepts were introduced, developers' presentations depicted magnificent coloured drawings, lots of people buying, pretty girls on bicycles, restaurants busy and filled with ravenous customers, everybody out with nothing else to do. In the drought of left-overs from the barren years after the war we were happy to get anything.

We forgot that people come in many guises. And we were disappointed when our beautiful people malls for beautiful ladies and their fashion shops actually turned out to be the last resort for those who have no homes. The developers' presentations of coloured drawings did not translate into the stink and chaos of the real thing and we are disappointed. Forgotten in those drawings were the people who can be so different from ourselves and we can hardly bear the sight of them.

People places must be for everyone—is how we started out. Sometimes "everyone" is not like ourselves and that was not grasped at the time. That our paved and boulevarded malls become havens for people different from ourselves, heaven forfend. Of course, we all like people, but the malls and streets that started out as beautiful drawings but did not turn out that way, are declared to be a disgrace, havens of drug dealers, congregating places for skinheads and rockers, hang outs for the rubbies. Ultimately, they run down and become neglected. We let them run down. Merchants have a hard time promoting their stores. They're bad for business. And the big and beautiful one-stop, limitless parking palaces in the suburbs take our attention and our money. The poor old inner city malls dwindled. Or so we thought.

We learn the hard way, of course. Years before the pedestrian mall became *au courant* no one dreamed a street was anything other than a place to go about our daily business. The street worked; traffic went through; people got out to shop as best suited their purpose and the town was alive. Whoever used the street could be accepted on their own terms. Malls and beautification were far from our civic minds.

One of the first street malls, or to be more precise,

back-alley malls to be developed was in Victoria. At the
time, although little used and much unnoticed, it was quite
an innovation. Trounce Alley was designed in 1954 by
this author and John Wade. Back then Trounce Alley was a
not-so-significant, privately owned, right of way behind the
Royal Trust Building, between Government Street and Broad
Street. And because the private owners wanted to maintain
their legal ownership, each year for a day the alley is barri-
caded off. A commissionaire guards the street entrances and
the public, in order to pass through, asks permission. No one
was ever denied. And the little mall prospered.

The large presence of the eight-storey Royal Trust Building was on the south side and a few innocuous little shops and
a café occupied the other side of the alley. The lane was *133*
used as a pedestrian throughway but its potential for shopping remained untapped. Once redesigned, the alley became
renowned throughout Victoria. When once dressed up, instead of letting it languish as a short cut for the hurried and
distracted, it became a modest little pedestrian mall. And so it
is today, essentially in the same form as when I designed it in
1954. Trounce Alley was possibly the first forgotten alley-way
to have been developed into a pedestrian mall, in this country,
in the post-war era.

Only some years later did the city street take hold in the
public imagination. In the early 1960s in Great Britain, the
National Trust encouraged the beautification of Magdallen
Street, Norwich, to the thunder of international applause.
Then Jane Jacobs got the ball rolling on the North American
continent with her quaint nostalgic image of the local street:
the butcher, the baker and the kids playing with the fire hy-
drant on a hot summer day. Years later the images percolated
into the slowly ruminating Canadian minds and Lothian
Mews, in Yorkville, Toronto was built. From then on, the
great surge of the shopping mall couldn't be held back.

Still, long before the pedestrian mall was sanctified as a
marketing and sociological necessity, there have always been
well-worn pedestrian throughways that people have used for
generations. They were the shopping streets of the traditional
city. Not all of them have been treated like Trounce Alley,
but they have been firmly rooted in the economic activities of
their respective cities, unnoticed and appreciated. These
throughways come out of necessity. Necessity pre-dated
market research. The patterns they formed came from an

unconscious response, following habits, responding to clearly defined needs of the day. The pattern these throughways etched are especially evident in the older cities. St. John's has a few of them.

St. John's is where it all started 400 years ago, the British North American presence, that is, not the malls. So they have had a head start when it came to finding pathways through their town. The street pattern of St. John's follows the length of the contours of the hills skirting the harbour. Pedestrian steps and pathways cross connect. For obvious reasons the streets follow the easy grade, leaving the steep part for pedestrian steps. McMurdo Steps is typical of this response to hills and harbour, for it climbs from Water Street to climax in the most necessary watering hole, the Duke of Duckworth. So many pilgrims wend their inevitable way to the Duke of Duckworth at the top, that estimating the value of McMurdo Steps to the overall economy of St. John's cannot be overblown. Undoubtedly, they are the driving reason for the well-being of that once great seaport on the eastern seaboard.

Another great seaport on the eastern seaboard also has a traditional street layout, directed by the slope of the land to the harbour. The port is Halifax. The streets of Halifax follow spatial patterns signifying the economy of the times. Brick warehouses, dock facilities and sandstone office buildings centre around the working port. Close, up the hill, the commercial city centre reflects the maritime origins.

The port has shifted now and the port-related city has had to find another purpose. Old industrial buildings, port-related work places, have now been converted to other uses. Old brick and sandstone offices and warehouses have been painted up and renovated. Dock buildings have been converted into commercial tourist attractions, with a new name—Historic Properties.

Up the hill a block, away from the waterfront, Halifax has its mall, too, on Granville Street, figure **100.** In the area of renovated buildings between the Historic Properties and downtown, **46,** one short block, the mall shows off a fine reuse of the old facades. Inside, behind the facades, and above the stores are just two uses. One is the Nova Scotia College of Art and, the other, the Barrington Hotel. A variety of shops and restaurants occupy the mall fronts. Shops, restaurants and pubs line both sides. Some of the restaurants seat their customers out on the street paving in the summer. The paved

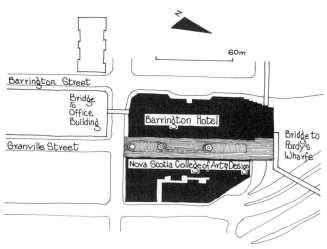

60m

Barrington Street

Bridge
to
Office
Building

Barrington Hotel

Granville Street

Nova Scotia College of Art & Design

Bridge to
Purdy's
Wharf

135

Figure 100. Granville Mall   Halifax   N.S.

surface is furnished with benches, flower tubs, and fountains.
The mall is short and the unique mix of buildings, the college,
the hotel, the shops and restaurants gives it a more than
ephemeral distinction.

There is no traffic. The mall is devoted entirely to pedestrians. Yet activity is gregarious. The crowds flock at recognizable times, in summer, on weekends, and not surprisingly
when the pubs open. At other times, the place is dead. Some
of the time, lots of people mill around: noise, jostling, chatter,
then boom, there isn't a soul in sight. How this works out for
the merchants is hard to tell without talking to every one of
them. But like so many malls across the country, Granville
Mall, Halifax, is an attraction for a brief period, usually at midday, during the tourist season. Flashing moments of vigorous
activity then quiet and becalm. Saturday nights, the restaurants are crowded and the noise from the music is ear rend-
ing. Monday morning the rent has to be paid.

How much the seasonal tourist trade can help a downtown place come alive is a deep and closely guarded secret.
Talk to the merchants and they will tell you things are perennially bad. Talk to the tourist promotion office and they will
tell you their glossy promo literature is drawing people from
Tierra del Fuego, rain is liquid sunshine and everything is
let's have a party. A glance at the empty store fronts, a look at

who survives the winter or a record of tenant turnover is, however, a giveaway. And generally that supports the merchants' point of view.

But the controversy is not unique to Halifax. Does beautification and surface splendour transform into lasting benefits?. Who knows? Experience shows that the pretty-coloured renovations and historic reinterpretations last a while, then the tourists get bored and move elsewhere. Tourists have a short attention span. There is little of substance in the repetitive, everybody is doing it, environment of superficial rehabilitation. The Jane Jacobs gone overboard, the sated farmers' markets, the sham historic regurgitations have all but run their course. One day the little guy who invests all his savings is going to tumble to the fact.

One thing is easy to see, nevertheless. All the activity in Historic Properties and Granville Mall put together are no match for the real activity going on all day, every day, all-year-round up the hill on Spring Garden Road. That street really lives up to its name.

Spring Garden Road, **101,** is on the other side of downtown from Granville Mall, five blocks westward. To get there you pass Province House and those dead, victorious soldiers celebrating Mafeking, Krugersdoorp (now that's public art for you), then on. Spring Garden starts on Barrington, at the cemetery, and goes up the hill, past the university, past Churchill brooding in the library garden, past the park and up to

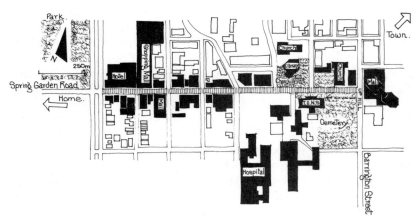

Figure 101. Spring Garden Road

where everyone lives. And it is the stream of people moving past these places to where they live that makes the street so spirited.

But that isn't all. In the six short blocks of commercial activity, the surroundings comprise a hospital, technical university, library, church, the Lord Nelson Hotel, the park and the thousands of people living close by. With such a mix of contiguous activity, so many residents, so many passers-by through each day, to and from work, how can the street be other than successful? And it is this understanding of the underpinning of a good urban street that is lacking in all the malls and Historic Properties no matter how much is spent on slick handouts.

On the way home everyone passes the shops; that is the *137* secret of Spring Garden Road's success. What is enervating on the mall?—no movement. What is energizing to the atmosphere of the street ?—movement, slow velocity movement, coarse grain movement, and congestion. Movement past the shops and all the surrounding activities marks the difference between the street and the mall.

Singling out the endeavours of Halifax to improve and resuscitate old unused buildings hide a picture plethora of cities all chasing the same dream. What is said for Halifax can well apply to other cities. Malls, shopping malls all over the city hides a superficial understanding of what makes the modern city tick. That is indeed the tragedy. Our imaginations have failed us. So far, we can do no better than follow the leader to stagnation and a dream of success, pontificated by promo literature.

Québec, within the walls, is an animated historic renovation ferment. Mall titivation is not necessary when every structure is a potential place to paint pretty, install a chef and cook it up. In the winter, inside the walls, the grey granite buildings cast a different presence. All is sombre in the ecclesiastical quiet, closed up, protected from the the snow and cold. But, unsuspected in the winter, the summer transforms the quiet grey to a glow. In grey winter crevices, the summer blossoms into colour. What in the winter was closed, blank, uninhabited and uninviting, turns into inviting summer restaurants, artists' displays, performers, dancers, jugglers.

Outside the walls where the real people live, life continues all year long. And to sustain it they have created a weather-enclosed mall that extends for blocks. Mall Centre-

Ville, fully enclosing rue Notre-Dames-des-Anges runs six
blocks long just west of the big Dufferin freeway. The mall
is a street enclosed with a plastic skylight top. In the enclosure there are stores, a church—Église St-Roch—many
restaurants and a full commercial array of activities. It is
a street-long shopping centre, running in the densely populated part of the city.

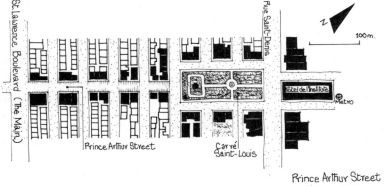

Prince Arthur Street
Figure 102.

Prince Arthur Street, **102,** in Montreal, is a mall of a different sort. Not weather enclosed, although the winter weather is no less harsh than in Québec, Prince Arthur Street is
busy. How well the restaurants are patronized on a dark No-
vember night is hard to estimate, but they appear crowded.
A winter's day is like a summer's day, there are so many
people living close to the shops and restaurants, they cannot
help but use them. The place is busy all the time. Summertime particularly, is active and the activity is not confined to
business hours.

Prince Arthur Street Mall is continuous, if carré St-Louis
can be included, all the way from the Sherbrooke metro station to St. Lawrence, The Main, some eight blocks. Along and
around the mall, the area is crowded with densely occupied
houses, apartments, rooming houses and people living and
working. No wonder the place is busy. St. Lawrence, itself, is a
well established shopping street. It feeds Prince Arthur in a
way that their attractions complement one another.

Maybe this is an opportune moment to make a statement
about the viability of downtown, in view of successful Prince
Arthur Street. Titivating, tarting up tacky old districts means

nothing if there lacks a dense base population of people of all incomes: families, singles, rich and poor. People living in an affordable downtown, working, shopping, enjoying life free from debt, noise and pollution in a pleasant environment is the single overriding issue that faces the development of the modern Canadian city. Beautiful public urban space is the key to pleasant, dense living downtown and that's what this book is all about. Street beautification, paving, planting or other shallow hype will not make up for that. Over the years there's been lots of talk, not much action—now let's see something done about it!

The area, Prince Arthur that is, has been the same for years. Some modern buildings stand out above the rest but not intrusively. The residential buildings are solid, well cared for and, around Carré St. Louis, expensive. Carré St-Louis was as recently as 1980 a place for the poor to live. There appears to have been a major shift in the pattern for now the area is an upbeat community.

Montreal is big. Evidently 60,000 people live in the downtown area. Retail intensity on Prince Arthur Street has had no damaging effect on the business on St. Catherine Street or The Main, at all, as though anyone would believe it would. Montreal has so much vitality, many activity areas can prosper simultaneously; that cannot be said for many other cities whose aspiring malls go bust. Within that vitality there is room for many active streets. And that significant detail is lost on the smaller cities which emulate the patterns of the larger centralized power places without understanding the underlying principles of intense activity. Big cities develop malls ad infinitum. Smaller cities should be more selective.

Likewise, intense activity on Yonge and Bloor Streets in Toronto is, if anything, complemented by the magnetic draw of Yorkville, despite the regressive effect Eaton's galleria has had on the lower end of Yonge. Big city activity encourages activity. The many centres of activity on Queen West can also sustain the proliferation of shopping malls around it. On the other hand, intense activities on Granville Island, in Vancouver, and cloned farmers markets all over did not help Gastown and, unnoticed, the strong street activity shifted to Denman Street.

But to return to Prince Arthur Street. Prince Arthur Street mall offers a classical opportunity for mall *aficionados* to discover what makes a good mall work. Success is not depen-

139

dent on any one class of business. No one type of space dominates the other. Small scale is evenly distributed along the length. Nor is it dependent upon being called a bus mall, a transit mall or a pedestrian mall, although it clearly is the latter. Its success comes from it being a sensibly included piece of the community that surrounds it and being crossed by a vital shopping street, The Main. Everyone is working; it is a classy neighbourhood. Purposeful people can almost be taken for granted. Success on the street comes from the relatively coarse grain social mix of people living in the area.

That is more than can be said for Sparks Street Mall in Ottawa. For although Ottawa has residential accommodation in the downtown there does not seem to be enough people to keep the place active after hours.

Sparks Street Mall is four long blocks. The Bank of Canada presents one dreary glass wall along the face of one length of block on the western end. The mall terminates at the eastern end at Confederation Square. In between the bank and Confederation Square there are thirteen banks, too many government offices, not enough variety to attract activity after hours. Traffic home from the Houses of Parliament precinct and other work locations crosses its flow rather than moving along it. It is by-passed by its most important clientele. No one pauses; it is inconvenient and there is nothing to stop for. Bank Street farther south takes the extended business activity leaving Sparks Street Mall high and dry.

140

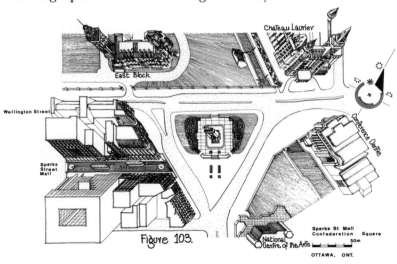

Figure 103.

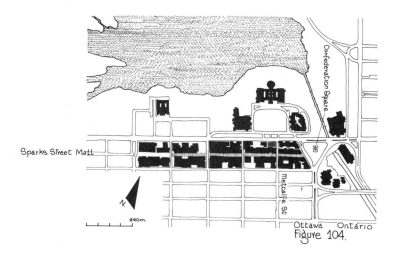

Sparks Street Mall

Confederation Square

Metcalfe St

Ottawa   Ontario
Figure 104.

141

Confederation Square, **103,** is an amorphous mass of left over semi-urban space drenched in snarled up traffic, centred on the inevitable memorial to dead soldiers. On the map the place is grand when in reality it is noisy, dangerous and full of confusing traffic for pedestrians. The Mall, **104,** starts at the blank Bank of Canada, runs through stark bureaucracies, and ends up in confusion at Confederation Square. If ever there was a recipe for a moribund street, Sparks Street Mall has it.

Nevertheless during certain peak hours there is some activity. In summer, during the day, well over 13,000 pedestrians, appendix III, have been counted. In the winter, at the same time, 2,000 pedestrians have been counted. That activity, however, is confined mostly to the lunch hour peak period. During the remaining daylight hours very little happens.

The mall is the centre-piece of downtown. Supposedly it is the main attraction for a revitalized central area. Yet it cannot compete with all the other attractions, By Ward market, Rideau Street and more. Ottawa downtown is saturated in modern shopping malls and retail places, to say nothing of the replicated facilities in the suburbs.

Renovations to Sparks Street Mall were being carried out during the summer of 1987. Time will show how much these renovations will meet the needs of the merchants. But questions persist—what can paving, lamp standards, glass shelters and planting do to make up for insufficient population living close by, too many single use buildings and nothing particularly attractive to lure people back after lunch? The lesson of Prince Arthur Street Mall is that the people should not be lured back, they should be living there to start with.

People don't need lunch-time to get them to Transit Terminus Mall in Saskatoon. Saskatoon has taken advantage of having a small, interesting and active downtown. Indeed, most activity occurs on Thursdays when the Mennonites come to town. But farmers and residents alike arrive in the city all the time, any day of the week, and Transit Terminus, **105,** is the central point from where the Saskatoon bus service brings them to and fro.

_142_

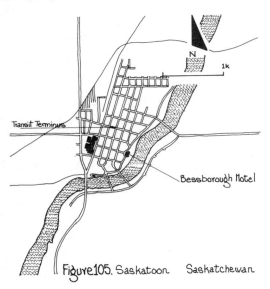

Figure 105. Saskatoon   Saskatchewan

That one short block is effective. Small as it may be the activity is intense. Buses come in droves all day. The pavements are wide to handle alighting and boarding passengers. Enclosing buildings, those facing onto the mall, are one storey and generally small in scale, appropriate for the walking public. Passengers patronize the many small and unpretentious shops and restaurants. Clearly the mall is an important centre for the commercial activity of downtown Saskatoon.

In contrast, Scarth Street Mall in Regina, **28,** is quiet. Most of the day, even in fine weather, few people are attracted. It should be busier being connected to two well, used areas, Victoria Park and the Cornwall shopping centre. Cornwall Centre is the largest downtown shopping facility. Victoria Park is a beautiful, treed oasis surrounded by small office buildings, shops and hotels.

Scarth Street Mall, with its contiguous amenities, is Regina's centre. The paved surface runs north and south. Stores, two-and-three storey buildings line the length. The old post office with its neighbouring theatre front shows off a significant texture heritage facade at the north end of the mall. The southern gateway to the mall, opening onto Victoria Park, will one day be fixed by two glass towers, each about fifteen stories high. Today only one is built.

Intended to be the generator of the downtown rejuvenation, the rejuvenated rail yards are yet to be developed. The proposed development is to be to the north, on the other side of the Cornwall Centre. Regina is yet another urban *143* centre that will be the heir to a large tract of inner city land left when the railway marshaling yards are relocated. But for now Scarth Street Mall languishes awaiting its potential.

Steven Avenue Mall in Calgary, **106,** may well languish too, now the Olympic Games are over. Much of the mall was sacrificed to build the Olympic Plaza. And Calgary is yet another city reliant upon the commuter for its downtown life. When the commuter goes home for the evening so does Calgary.

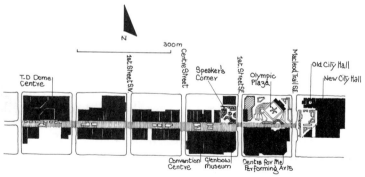

Figure 106. Steven Avenue Mall   Calgary Alta

Steven Avenue Mall runs east to west for five blocks from Calgary City Hall to the business centre. For most of its length modest shop fronts (from the days of the street) line either side. Few looming buildings dominate; for the most part the scale is compatible with the pedestrian. Past 1st Street the scale abruptly changes. No longer are there small-scale shops—large buildings, the museum and the performing arts centre assume predominance. Grand scale takes over. Speaker's Corner slices off what was once a sharp and satisfying street corner and grey concrete diffuses the light. The museum interrupts the tempo. Scale, the way of comprehending for the pedestrian, disappears.

Olympic Plaza past Speaker's Corner defaults to fractionated chunks of surface left over from the hallelujah days of winning and medals. The plaza was great in the dark of those winter nights, so many lights, so much excitement, so many people. But when the games were over the feeling of the space reverted to built-in ennui.

The plaza is lost in a diaspora of split surfaces and noisome streets. The very important line that defines all urban space, the infinitesimal strip joining the vertical building facade to horizontal pavement surface is unnoticeable, lost in the melee of chaotic surroundings. Confused pergolas like piled kindling, pointed towers like ghost town gravestones litter the views and vistas. Everywhere the prospect is of surface running out of surface until finally the viewer is confronted by the bland and faceless City Hall. Reflecting, mocking, the front of the City Hall slips away to where it's going, nowhere.

Steven Avenue is another lunch-time mall. Midday, the brief period when business is booming the mall is alive. Bands play, outdoor restaurants feed, people stroll, the place is a mass of activity, texture, lots of colour, commerce and smells. I enjoyed a long afternoon browsing the mall in the spring of 1987, the year before the games. The weather was beautiful. I bustled to the best spot, close enough to hear, where the noisy rock concert is dampened. The sun rang in with warmth and welcome. The only shade was under the coloured umbrellas. Buildings are not so high, for most of the length, so as to crowd out the sunshine. I stayed on the mall all afternoon.

I watched the people come and go. Isn't that what the mall is for? One man who seemed to be important stood out beyond the crowd. Grey-suited, tie and shirt, incongruous on this hot day the man passed up and down the mall, exchanging friendly greetings with the people.

And, as the afternoon wore on, the lunch-time crowd dispersed, the lunch-time bustle went with it. A change of pace occurred. Another group took over, sparser this time. In no rush, just hanging about the store fronts, out they came, chatting, relaxing, sun bathing. Who were they? The question arises especially when the important man stopped all the time to chat with them. Of course they were the shopkeepers. They had no business after the noontime crowd had gone. So they enjoyed the sunshine. The important man returned to the bank on the corner. He was their local banker, giving his friendly advice no doubt. The day was long gone. The banker looked after business. Mall life can be agreeable at times.

Not everyone agrees. If business has a hard time surviving and undesirables frequent the mall, as gossip would have it, why have so many malls been built? Why do we persist in keeping them plodding along? I have frequented almost every major mall in the country. No doubt about it I have smelled the people, some of them are not so sweet. Possibly nefarious deals were conducted right under my nose, for I am too ingenuous to notice. But never have I been hassled, remotely inconvenienced or put at risk. Problems exist to be sure, but malls are a new phenomenon, as urban spaces become acceptable. In time we'll learn to use them. For, in their present form, the generic outdoor urban mall is preferable to the too ubiquitous, plastic, pink plastered, air-conditioned, subterranean wasteland that masquerades as the shopping centre that destroys our sense of city now.

145

Granville Mall in Vancouver typifies the perennial discussion of the generic mall and its success—or lack of it. For years, Vancouver has lamented its scruffy demise. For years they have looked for remedies.

Granville Mall, **107,** was laid out in the early 1970s. The new council of that time wanted to bring life back to the inner city. Not that life had left; still, it just wasn't the pretty

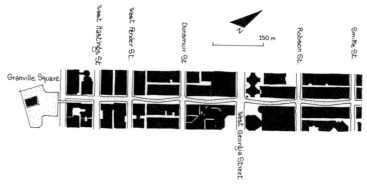

Figure 107.   Granville Mall   Vancouver B.C.

looking stuff of the magazine covers. And in typical Canadian fashion off they traipsed for a junket to Minneapolis to check out Nicolette Mall. They returned with a transit mall idea: lots of people, only buses, taxis and a winding road to slow speed down.

The reason for the installation of the mall: conventional wisdom had Granville Street becoming seedy, the new Pacific Centre had just been built, something had to be done to bring life to the street. And, as the mall was being paved, two other large interruptions were happening at the Georgia intersection. The new Birks Scotia Tower was going up with the IBM Centre shortly after. And, of dire consequence to the street activity, the centres were connected underground with a brand new shopping plaza.

146

Pacific Centre underground was already syphoning customers away from the streetside shops on Granville Street. Pacific Centre runs parallel to Granville Street and instead of complementing the activity on the street it is a very strong attraction away from it. Eaton's galleria does the same to Yonge Street in Toronto despite its alleged similarity to the galleria in Milan.

The best use of enclosed city malls such as the Pacific Centre in Vancouver and Eaton's galleria in Toronto is for them to act as connecting links between street level attractions. This way they enjoy busy crowds within their enclosures but they do not do so at the expense of the established retail activities on the street outside. A well placed enclosed shopping mall can be a decisive asset to the street activities surrounding it.

So, regardless of the effects of Pacific Centre, a design for Granville Mall that encouraged patterns of activity to help smaller business prosper was envisioned. Justifiable as it was, it was not enough. For the underground Pacific Centre in the end had a profound effect on the street activity for some time to come. The mall languished for fifteen years.

Comparisons were inevitably made with Robson Street, **29,** which is a very popular retail strip that, together with Denman Street, rivals Yonge Street, Toronto, as a never-ending display of people, shops and urban life. As Granville Mall became more drab, Robson Street thrived. Thank God no one had the bright idea of making it the mall. For Robson Street (like Spring Garden Road in Halifax) is a going concern of much different urban circumstance to Granville Street.

Robson Street combines a trendy shopping street with a coarse-grained traffic thoroughfare from downtown to the suburbs. Starting downtown, where people work, it continues into the most populated part of the town, the West End, then beyond. People walk home from work, they drive home to West Vancouver, and they stop on the way in the stores. For on their way a variety of shops, restaurants, the Art Gallery, the sunken Robson Square attract attention.

Despite the popularity of Robson street, Granville Mall is doing a little better now. You can't hold a good place down for long. Unnoticed amidst the lamentations that the mall was failing, patterns changed and business grew. Old, tacky head shops remain; strip joints and beer halls persist, but their drab condition is limited. A new vitality spans beyond the lunch hour; Granville Mall never was a lunch-hour mall in any case, and gradually the tackiness was eclipsed by the new-found energy. Fortunately, despite fears of imminent demise, no precipitous action was taken to dismantle Granville Mall. Instead, it enjoys a face-lift.

As a part of Granville Mall, theatre row prospers. Night and day the place is humming. Cineplex Odeon surreptitiously shows off Jack Shadbolt's mural behind a candy counter. (Another Jack Shadbolt, *Butterflies*, not on the mall, can be seen in Mac Blo's lobby. And with Michael Snow's *Geese* in Toronto, these pieces have to be some of the best public art in Canada.)

Inner city urban malls came out of a well-intentioned urge to bring the city back to the people. The streets that were there all the time became too familiar. We got too used to them. In our familiarity, we lost sight of what they meant to us.

In our mixed up priorities parking the car became more important. We have misunderstood the impact of the car. Fear of change has instilled in the merchants a resistance, even if it is for the better. Someone has told them if the car isn't parked in front of their store, they'll lose business. They forget that if it parks too long they'll lose business too. The line drawn between vigorous vehicular traffic for shoppers and the insidious, free-standing commercial parking on every corner is fine. We have uncritically taken the numbers of the traffic engineer as gospel. Entrenched commuter traffic demands inevitably take priority. The inner workings of the city are far more complex than traffic numbers, yet we have given way to their dictatorial, one-dimensional, simplistic calculations.

147

We made unreasonable comparisons with the well-ordered suburban shopping palaces. Downtown is not comparable to the suburbs. Indeed, we came to expect too much of the downtown. We have designed our malls with an agenda beyond the boundaries of their space and far beyond the influence of their economic capabilities. We thought we could bring instantaneous success and vigour to a run down area by just fixing up the paving. We forgot the streets have been the generators of economic activity for generations, at least streets similar to those previously mentioned, Spring Garden Road and Robson Street. Shops on the streets sprung up out of need. On our malls the shops sprung up in the hopes they would attract a need.

148

Because they are economically contrived, so many of the intentionally designed malls do not fare well. Installed with a purpose to rejuvenate an inner area, the malls are marooned in a derelict part of town where few people live, where few want to live and where many are leaving. Surrounding development is held up by fictitious land prices, ever-rising for no apparent market reason, held in the grip of a financier's poker game that no one else can join.

Some streets have been arbitrarily chosen as the victims of beautification for the purpose of gentrifying the neighbourhood. Victims they are, for the merchants are assessed, supposedly, for improvements that seldom give back an equitable benefit. Or, they are chosen for the heritage nature of the buildings. And the heritage buildings are located out of the swim of habitual economic activity and their location is ill-suited to their new purpose.

Despite these shortfalls, for a time, some of the malls prosper. Newness, novelty and publicity draws a host of out-of-towners. Then, when the novelty wears thin, the old shopping habits return. The mall goes quiet and the best situated streets return to normal.

Generically, we have attributed far greater urban regenerating powers to malls than so far they seem to have demonstrated. Without the dense population of the surrounding inner city residents, there can be no sustained prosperity. Often forgotten in the rush to revitalize the centre is the magnetic influence of the suburban shopping centres. Inner city malls cannot compete. Indeed, the drawing power of the massive shopping centre is not forgotten, it is ignored. So, with the outer ring booming, the inner space goes quiet. And, predictably, out trots the idea of paving the streets, boulevarding the sidewalks, dressing up the store fronts and putting in bicycle racks. Locally, a sense of satisfaction in having at least done something blinds us to the fact that what had been done is not producing results for the merchants on the streets.

Speaking *sotto voce* to city planners in their offices one will invariably be told of a general lack of trading activity in the mall shops. Mention of this aloud is considered to be bad for the tourist trade yet we go on in our merry way building these things, beautifying, not admitting failures, letting people in for disappointment after they have unloaded their life savings into small retail businesses.

To understand, completely, the influences that make a downtown work let alone what makes a mall or a street work is not a scientific exercise. As knowledge expands, the conditions shift. What can be seen in one set of circumstances as economic issues become cultural issues in other circumstances. Our penchant for separating the elements of the city into manageable portions is confounded by the irrevocable interrelationship of the parts. But one thing does stand out, a busy prosperous commercial area tends to give itself vitality, give itself an attractive atmosphere and tends to police itself. What makes business successful cannot be replicated by tarting up a few benches, planters and cross walks. The changes have to be profound.

If we would accept the original purpose of the inner city, that is, as a place to attain satisfaction from work, some progress may be made. Instead of looking to the city as the place to spend money we should look to it as the place to create wealth, not paper wealth, real wealth. Somewhere to go to work. Work is not just paper shuffling or short order cooking; work produces material benefit to the whole community. We should look to the city as somewhere we can afford to live so we don't waste all day commuting, waiting for someone ahead to move, landing up exhausted with little energy left to get on with the job.

149

7

Havens and Harmony

150 Saving old buildings concentrates our energy so completely we lose sight of the essential purpose in the city. Heritage preservation is the easy way out. We have made a subliminal decision to abandon the creation of an urban environment in our own unique vision, complementing but not imitating the past. Are we unrealistically superimposing on the past an unattainable mythical quality? Are we bent on reliving the past as an escape from the present? Is heritage preservation escapism?

The essential purpose of city design is to create harmonious, reposeful spaces best suited to our living and working customs now. Gussying up a few old warehouses with a superficial paint job, converting them to a purpose for which they were never intended, and hailing them as great stuff is no way to direct our contemporary energy. That is not city design.

Invariably the buildings we struggle so hard to save are mediocre architecture—hardly our most precious architectural heritage. Yet, we save what we can for sentimental reasons. Our sentiments for buildings would be better directed towards our fellow human beings, if betterment of the environment of the city is to be the end result. Some of us are old enough to remember these heritage buildings in their working days. They were no more revered, then, than we respect our own now. Sometimes, we will fight to save anything just because it's old. Heritage preservation is politically popular at the expense of the overall urban environment.

We make the urban environment (or at least our way of looking at it) so complex the issues have become diffused as to be almost unmanageable. Selected issues, such as heritage conservation, are treated ad nauseam, with a good show of civic concern. However, they are smoke screens deflecting attention from substantial issues. Planning conditions we want to put forward, affordable housing, amenable public urban space, are lost. Such conditions are difficult to achieve so we make do.

Heritage is but one issue, yet we have made it the crutch to lean all our weight upon. Traditional architectural heritage and customs, of course, must be preserved, not as caricatures of their noble past, but as going concerns. Believe me, our way of doing business today is not that different from the recent past. We should preserve them in their original capacity. They are an inventory from which we measure values we profess to hold in trust.

Old buildings are all very fine so long as they are preserved for a substantial purpose. If economic theory determines that perfectly sound, usable, albeit old, buildings have outlived their value then perhaps we should revalue economics. There are instances where old, yet sound affordable apartment buildings have been demolished to make way for expensive condominiums. In Vancouver forty-two affordable apartments were demolished to make way for twenty-two expensive condominiums that will probably remain empty on a saturated market for some time. In Montreal, the Sherbrooke Apartments have been replaced by the museum addition. In such instances heritage makes more than good sense.

On the other hand, we don't have to look far to find dormant urban areas of beautiful old buildings spruced up into retail malls with the tenants desperately trying to look busy. What is the point of heritage preservation in those instances? The point is to divert our attention from more substantive, more compelling, yet more politically contentious development that would do more good.

All of the above are happening in every city, every day. There must be a useful arbiter of purpose for us to decide what makes a valuable heritage building. Surely, there can be no better purpose for the preservation of heritage architecture than for it to chart the course of our civic development— for us to declare, through the medium of our architecture, how we have arrived at where we are. Implicit in that purpose, then, is a reinterpretation of how we use the preserved buildings. If we trivialize our heritage architecture by making perfectly sound structures into tacky little markets, boutiques, gift shops and painted fronts, chances are we are trivializing

151

ourselves. If we cannot find a better purpose, then our imagination and courage must have surely left us.

The way we develop the city is a reflection of the way we see ourselves; hence, the medium of architecture. Heritage architecture, although a vital enough issue on its own, is peripheral to the topic.

The architectural and urban design principles explained in the previous chapters are applied here to the following examples of real spaces, in real cities. Some of these instances include living heritage reconstructions. The others, three of them, are contemporary buildings: Maison Alcan, Montreal; Market Square, Toronto; and Gastown Square, Vancouver.

The three last-mentioned examples are all contemporary parts of the city integrated into the traditional fabric. They are not chunks of solid form imposed upon their neighbours like so many modern buildings are. They speak as sensitive and economically valuable pieces of urban vitality. The medium of their architecture is responsive to contemporary conditions. Their design demonstrates the best application of the principles of urban space. They represent spatial havens, in harmony with the bustling city.

Starting with living heritage reconstructions in Québec's old city, figure **108,** Québec is chosen, not because its heritage architecture, *l'architecture patrimoine,* is easy to enjoy, which indeed it is, but rather because the urban conglomera-

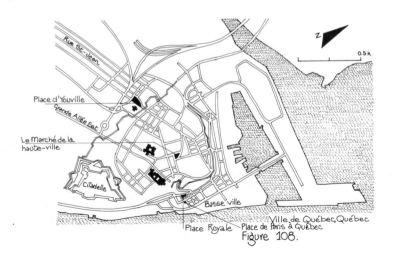

Place d'Youville
Rue St-Jean
Grande Allée Est
Le Marché de la haute-ville
Citadelle
Basse ville
Place Royale   Place de Paris à Québec
Ville de Québec, Québec
Figure 108.
0.5 k

tion of old Québec is an educational experience as well as an
enjoyable one. Many of the heritage renovations are buildings
used for their original purposes. Edifice Price is one such heritage building. Well designed on the alignment of rue Saint-
Anne, Edifice Price is used as an office building, virtually
unchanged from when it was built fifty years ago.

The old city is replete with urban space reconstructions,
similar to but older than Edifice Price. (Reconstructions are
old buildings that have been given a new and useful life, albeit
following their original purposes.) The Séminaire and Basilique, were built in the seventeenth century for the purpose to
which they are used today. Hôtel de Ville was built in the last
century and is still in use. Many shops were built in the last
century, as shops, and are presently in use as the same. All of
these buildings are on one place in the old city, le Marché de
la haute-ville. Le Marché de la haute-ville is not some kind of
market renovation. It does not depend on a capricious redefinition of its use. It is what it was, what it is!

Le Marché de la haute-ville is the central urban space of
the old city. For urban beauty it is hard to surpass. Four streets
converge within its midst, **109.** This is a public urban space
that is an active, heritage space imbued with a contemporary
usefulness beyond the summer tourist trade. It is a public
urban space useful to the community, winter and summer.

The buildings surrounding Le Marché de la haute-ville,

153

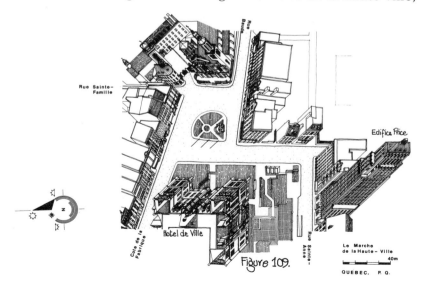

Figure 109.

Basilique, Le Marché de la haute-ville
Figure 110.

109, are, reading from the north east, the top left hand corner of the drawing, the Séminaire, the Basilique de Notre-Dame, **110,** and across rue Buade, a commercial shopping street with lending library, book shop, café and department store. Edifice Price is the tall office building on the south side of rue Sainte-Anne, the immediate westerly neighbour of Hôtel Clarendon. Hôtel de Ville is the building enclosing the west face of the space. Clearly these buildings are not tourist renovations. Although le Marché is the epitome of heritage preservation, it is also a working urban space. For the functioning buildings are used for daily civic business, work, worship, shopping and living—winter and summer.

Furthermore, the space at work today and the accretion of new building continues, at all times respecting the alignment of the street and the shape of the public urban space. The work constructing the older surrounding buildings commenced in the 1600s, but the spatial concept they engender is still respected. The Séminaire and the Basilique were the first to be constructed in the 1600s. In the 1930s Edifice Price was built. Construction to the present day consists of paving and landscaping in the garden south of le Hôtel de Ville.

Old Québec City depends on the summer tourist trade but le Marché de la haute-ville is very much a local's precinct all year round. What a good example to demonstrate reconstructed living urban space! At the same time, the enclosing surfaces, the building facades, follow the principles of good urban space design outlined in the list of "The Elements of Urban Space" (p. 73).

The local contemporary architects of Québec, as is evident in their designs of the later buildings, have obviously respected the intended shared vision of urban space. Furthermore, there has been, evidently, no need for burdensome controls to carry through with the shared vision. Edifice Price, in the way it was designed onto the street alignment of rue Saint-Anne, demonstrates how a large structure, a high rise, can be integrated into an existing urban space and enclosed by buildings of various heights, provided certain sensitive requirements are respected.

Although there have been no recent intrusions into le Marché de la haute-ville since the 1930s, buildings were constructed at different times during the previous 200 years or more. A shared vision of space accreted over several centuries. The architects of previous centuries respected the shared vision formed by previous builders. All the subsequent additions followed the street alignment and the concept of the working space.

155

The twentieth century changed everything. Fortunately, le Marché was not affected. But elsewhere sensitive people who understood the value of the beautiful urban space were put on the defensive. Public urban spaces of obvious cultural importance, Dominion Square and place du Canada in Montreal for instance, **35,** were threatened by insensitive intruders. These same intruders, builders of the modern office towers, were unable to respect the beauty of the surroundings of which they themselves wished to be a part. These beautiful public urban spaces must be defended against marauding developers lest they impede even their own purposes. The modern builder spends millions on quality sites only to inadvertently destroy the very qualities for which he pays so dearly. Somewhere there is a lesson in this for architects and planners.

Old Québec is replete with beautiful public urban spaces. Two, other than le Marché, stand out. They are reconstructed in a manner at odds with their original use. The original use, of course, was associated with the port as was so much of old Québec. Now all that is left of a future for the city is attracting tourists during the summer. The two spaces were most useful in Basse Ville when the old port was flourishing, long before the turn of the century. Those days are gone now, so the tourist purpose is now in effect.

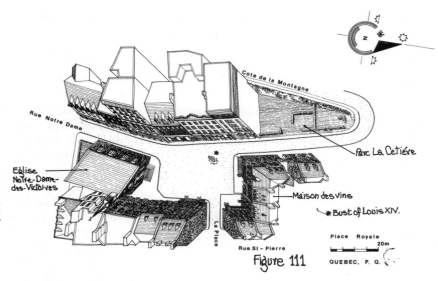

Figure 111

Place Royale, **111,** and place du Marché Finlay are the two urban spaces located in Basse Ville. Closely linked as an urban spatial couplet, they form a very compelling image of heritage urban space reconstructed with a contemporary connotation, the very important tourist business.

The two spaces have survived in one guise or another since the city was founded. The latter at the time of writing is still a parking lot. Old photographs show that our predecessors did not appreciate them with quite the same cultural point of view that we hold today. They were not revered as curious, but were taken for granted as hard working places in the commercial fabric, earning a living every day. Nevertheless, place Royale became an urban space of some significance after the fire of 1661. It was a working urban space after, too. Surrounding buildings were constructed to follow what were probably Canada's first urban design requirements. These requirements were the town planning regulations of Louis de Buade, Comte de Frontenac. He had a vision of Québec as the capital of New France in North America. He established design measures that set up street and space alignments for houses and other buildings, as well as fire precautions and regulations for cleanliness. His street alignment regulations preserved the present persistent space of place Royale.

Despite contemporary development pressures, that vision is upheld today. A most powerful new potential urban space is the proposed design for place du Marché Finlay by the Parisian artist Jean-Pierre Raynaud. If completed according to the design presentations, Québec will be the custodian of one of Canada's finest pieces of public urban art. The work of Raynaud will transform Finlay into la place de Paris à Québec.

Place du Marché Finlay is a short block east of place Royale, the two spaces are closely linked. The connection is strong, one can be seen from the other. Looking west from Finlay the bust of Louis XIV is visible in place Royale. A white marble stela visible from Royale, central to Finlay, will contrast with the ancient gray buildings now surrounding the parking lot.

Raynaud has designed a geometric public urban space, formed on sight lines, of eccentric geometry challenging our accustomed view of the old space. With a visibly strong personal statement in the form of a fixed centre, he has established visual axes that direct the view to the river. The fixed centre is a stela large in comparison to the human form, close-up, but intentionally ambivalent in relation to the scale of the space. The design re-defines the space by directing our attention with centripetal lines of spatial influence flowing with intensifying velocity, towards the centre-piece. Geometric paving describes a diagonal from the open waterfront towards the enclosing building surfaces on the landward side. The diagonal intersects two squares. One square is loaded with the stela, the other exhibits a paving pattern. The squares are eccentrically placed within a circle described in the paving. The stela is two marble blocks eccentrically piled, smallest atop the larger, squared off, lined and vividly etched.

In Canada, where public art is condescendingly inhibited by the caveat, do it for the people, this uncompromising personal redefinition of space is a glorious revelation. The piece can only be judged for the time being from the artist's presentation. The potential is there. Words cannot adequately describe what is by definition a spatial experience. The artist's description in his presentation is the only possible explanation for now. Leave words alone until the piece is completed.

Raynaud explains his spatial piece: *"Deux blocs très simples de marbre blanc, où seul le décalage de la partie haute évite la monotonie des concepts simplistes, réponse muette à l'espace, seule réponse que l'espace est en droit de recevoir".*

157

Successfully restored heritage urban spaces are familiar enough even when their beauty is less than in Québec. To an overweening extent we believe heritage places are the only beautiful urban spaces left for us in the compulsive world of modern city development. This is not always so. On occasion, we stumble into beautiful contemporary urban spaces enclosed by the most modern of architecture. Maison Alcan is one such place.

On Sherbrooke Street in the heart of Montreal's new business district, 1, Maison Alcan is a modern, corporate headquarters office building set into a block of traditional buildings. What a fine group of buildings it is! The new architecture merges with the traditional buildings so smoothly, the transition can hardly be felt. On Sherbrooke, the "wall alignment" has been upheld by accommodating much of the office space into five existing heritage facades. New and old mingle on the two flanking streets.

Maison Alcan is a remarkable group of buildings involving many qualities of urban space and urban building. One most encouraging aspect shows how contemporary architecture can be interwoven into the traditional city without losing modern convenience. For the space within these buildings is complex and simple at the same time. Space in Maison Alcan is a recursive experience. Recursive space is the art of weaving street space, enclosed public space, enclosed private space and open public space into a warp and weft of balanced complexity. The complexity makes for a sustained interest, unlike the you've seen one you've seen them all monotony of the usual office tower. The positive forms of the space merge with the solid forms of the buildings. Close weaves of forms evoke transparency and illusion similar to an Escher print, or the recursive continuity of a Bach fugue. The spaces flow together and they linger in the mind's eye long enough to form a continuous image. The images last as each spatial view is experienced separately. Then the experiences fold back into each other as continuous movement and light play showing off volume as a very stimulating effect.

Maison Alcan, insofar as it is a beautiful demonstration of how new buildings can create urban spaces that interweave the traditional customs and habits of the city and new patterns, belies our need to rely on heritage only to preserve the urban environment. The building group was designed by the late Ray Affleck and built in 1983. The same architect designed the

Confederation Centre of the Arts in Charlottetown, PEI, **21.**
Effusive praise for this building cannot go far enough.

Maison Alcan is in fact a group of eight buildings. The
group comprises the Davis Building, in which are the main
Alcan offices; five heritage Sherbrooke Street buildings, in
which are the Alcan executive offices and boutiques: and two
other buildings occupied by the Salvation Army, the office
tower on Stanley street, and the Citadel on Drummond
Street. Behind the heritage facades on Sherbrooke is a glass-
covered atrium enclosed by the Davis Building and the Sherbrooke buildings backing onto each other separated by the
few metres enclosing an atrium.

The footprint plan, **112,** illustrates as well as possible the
plan relationships between the solid forms and the positive
spaces. The five heritage buildings on Sherbrooke, marked
"renovations", and the Salvation Army Citadel are shown
in heavy diagonal hatching. The new Davis Building, fronting
on Drummond and Stanley, and the Salvation Army tower,
fronting on Stanley Street, are shown as solid black forms.
The atrium space between the Davis Building and the heritage renovations is shown in dotted diagonal hatching. The
open public spaces between these buildings is paved and
landscaped as gardens, lawns and pathways.

Maison Alcan on Sherbrooke Street, **113,** preserves and
complements the alignment of the Sherbrooke wall simply by
being there. The five heritage buildings of the complex are

159

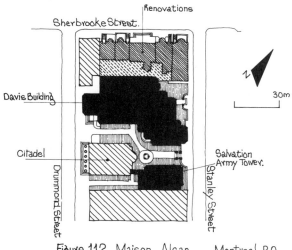

Figure 112. Maison Alcan   Montreal P.Q.

flanked on either side by two commercial, glass curtain-walled towers. The highest of the five Maison Alcan buildings, the middle heritage facade facing Sherbrooke, shown in **113,** was the Berkeley Hotel. The grey stone buildings on either side are what is left of nineteenth-century residential Montreal.

The Davis Building and the taller Salvation Army tower contrast with the older neighbours but do not compete for attention. Neither the architectural detailing nor the building heights vie for recognition. The design of the Alcan complex is powerful; yet, like all strong statements, its presence is not felt obtrusively. From Maison Alcan's simplicity comes strength.

160   Look through the arched portico on Stanley Street, **114,** into the inside urban space. From across the street a low sand-stone wall crosses over from the Salvation Army tower to, but not quite abutting, the Davis Building. The height of the wall fits a pedestrian's eye-level view. It is slightly alcoved for the entrance to the Davis Building. The colour and texture of the masonry is pleasant to see and to touch. Now move closer and see inside the off-street urban space. The new enclosing buildings, flanking both sides of the space, are clad in soft

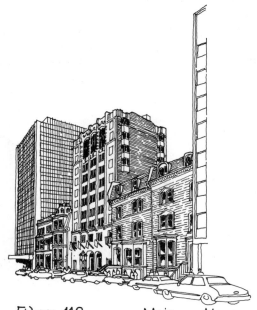

Figure 113.   Maison Alcan on Sherbrooke Street.

161

Figure 114. Maison Alcan on Stanley Street.

burnished aluminium panels set into a rectilinear pattern of horizontal and vertical dividers meticulously placed to etch a facade framework for the windows and the cladding panels as a unified wall surface.

The enclosed space between the Salvation Army and the Davis Building makes a slight shift as the garden path turns around the Citadel, **112,** and continues to connect with Stanley Street. Approaching the space from Drummond, **115,** is more direct. The view is uninterrupted for there is no portico, the permeability of the Stanley facade is transparently obvious. The Citadel is a low masonry solid form on the right. Masonry walls complement softly with the burnished aluminium of the Davis facade. The low Citadel does not block out the sun and the matt surface of the Davis Building reflects light gracefully. Complementary mellow materials enclose the space and have a moderating effect. The space is a microclimate of warm landscape, appreciated in late fall and very much in use in summer.

Through the medium of the traditional facades on Sherbrooke and the permeable qualities of the facades on Stanley and Drummond, Maison Alcan presents a thoughtful, neighbourly concern for the streets and citizens, and an acknowledgement to the city.

Acknowledgement of the city and public space are the hallmarks of a well-designed urban building. Maison Alcan

162

Figure 115.   Maison Alcan
on Drummond Street

meets all the criteria, and then some. So does Market Square in Toronto. Both share the architectural characteristic of a building that is shaped to enclose public space. Maison Alcan is an office building in downtown Montreal. Market Square is a residential and commercial building close to the reconstructed St. Lawrence Neighbourhood, **6,** and St. Lawrence Market in Toronto.

The St. Lawrence Market is a centre where farmers and shoppers have met almost since Toronto was the Town of York. The surrounding neighbourhood has been through a variety of transitions. In the early 1970s Toronto decided to create a new inner city residential neighbourhood. St. Lawrence Neighbourhood came into being. Ensuing development contiguous to, and encouraged by, the St. Lawrence Neighbourhood was the motivator that gave impetus to Market Square, situated just west across the road from St. Lawrence Market.

Market Square is the quintessential new urban building. Related closely to the traditional customs and surrounding older buildings, it is a new building reflecting contemporary indigenous architectural values and qualities of urban design. Constructed and completed in 1984, Jerome Markson was the architect. No part of Market Square touches a heritage building, yet the qualities of heritage architecture are well emulated within the contemporary design. Not that it looks like an old building, but rather it has all the qualities we admire in older buildings: street alignment, street colonade, scale, a hollow interior space and lots of small windows. Respect for heritage is apparent, for instance the subtle view of St. James spire on the axis of the interior courtyard. The spire is like an integrated mural on the axis of the enclosed public urban space formed by the wraparound buildings of Market Square.

On the footprint plan, **116,** Market Square shows in solid black. Two buildings show up as Market Square. Separating them is public space, the interior space, and a roof level garden space. Under the roof garden an open concourse provides access to retail and residential accommodation. The complex is mostly residential; about ten per cent of the volume is reserved for retail commercial activities. The public space continues from Front Street across the lane through the

163

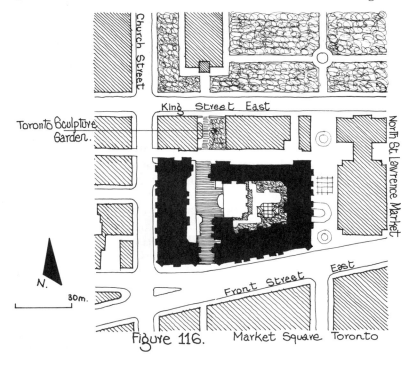

Figure 116.   Market Square Toronto

Toronto Sculpture Garden to King Street East. Buildings surrounding Market Square are diagonally hatched in the illustration. St. James Park across King Street East is scribble hatched and St. James Cathedral is diagonally hatched in the park. The illustration shows the manner in which the solid forms of the buildings wrap around the inner positive space, the public urban space. Outer surfaces of the buildings follow alignment of the surrounding streets.

Market Square is gently inserted into the neighbourhood. That is what makes it a successful urban building. In comparison to the neighbours it is not small, but it does not intrude, nor does it overshadow. North St. Lawrence Market next door by comparison is considerably less in volume and height, yet Market Square is a good neighbour.

164

Figure 117.   Market Square Toronto from Front Street.

Facades, **117,** are continuous around the four exposed sides. There is no doubting this is the same building, no matter from where it is approached, although there are fewer windows on the north facade overlooking the lane. Light buff masonry diffuses the strong, ubiquitous, overcast Toronto glare, contrasting the magenta masonry colouring of the attic storey. Market Square colour is bold and unequivocal. Yet because colour is inherent in the nature of the cladding materials, even though it is bold, it does not evoke an overpowering reaction—probably because natural colour in natural material, masonry, is not so dense as chemical colour. Natural colours can be used in larger and more intense architectural compositions.

Intervals between windows and projecting bay windows vary in metre and are of consistent proportions. Bay windows

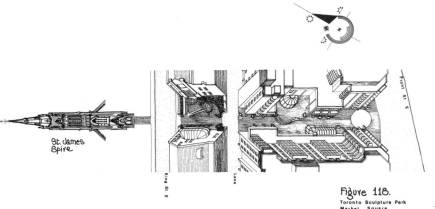

Figure 118.
Toronto Sculpture Park
Market Square
30m
TORONTO, ONT.

project a chiaroscuro shadow coinciding with the shadows caused by the permeability of the street level colonnade. The colonnade projects a horizontal shadow; bay windows project

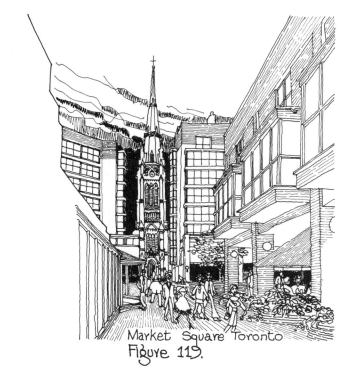

Market Square Toronto
Figure 119.

a vertical shadow. Light on the facade changes as the value of sunlight changes throughout the day, reflecting from the variety of architectural characteristics.

Public open space inside the complex, **118,** follows the visual axis of St. James's spire, **119.** Co-ordination of the space from Front Street East to the visual culmination of the spire comes out of a vision of urban space shared by Jerome Markson, the architect and Kenneth Greenberg who was, in the design phase, Toronto's urban designer. This spatial effect relies on three parts, the spire, the Toronto Sculpture Garden and the enclosed public space of Market Square.

Toronto Sculpture Garden is an integral part of the completed composition of Market Square. The relationship of the inside space wrapped around by Market Square and the garden is a beguiling experience. Market Square is a commercial place with restaurant tables and shops. The Sculpture Garden is host to changing events of artful design; you never know what to expect. There is something quite wonderful about the connection of these spaces that goes far beyond their small casual presence.

Market Place is eight stories at its highest, not a tall building but of some considerable volume. Width of the public spaces varies. Different roof levels of the enclosing architecture mitigates against an overpowering sense of size or closeness. Glass pavilions within the enclosed inside space relates height to a personal level.

Buildings surrounding the Toronto Sculpture Garden are three storeys high. Change in scale, from Market Square to Sculpture Garden is pleasant. Proportionate heights of the garden compared to the height of the Gothic-textured details of the slender spire come together and are very satisfying. Lines of spatial influence project from the spire into, and mingle reposefully with, the lines of spatial influence generated by enclosing surfaces of the Sculpture Garden and Market Square.

After Market Square and Maison Alcan the third example of contemporary architecture to which the principles of urban space are applied is Gastown Square in Vancouver. I hope that an image is appearing now of what to look for when trying to understand new buildings in the city, applying principles in the list of "The Elements of Urban Space" (p. 73). In addition to the elements, look for the overall spatial conception, the hollowed out shape within the complex itself. And it

_166_

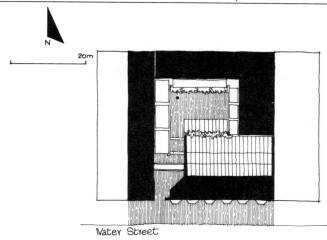

Water Street

Figure 120. Gastown Square Vancouver B. C.

gets more complicated because that hollowed out shape must be open to the public and it must be artfully connected to recursive space inside the building as well as the street.

Maison Alcan, Montreal, and Market Square, Toronto, meet the criteria of the other elements with panache. So does Gastown Square, Vancouver.

Gastown Square is a commercial retail and office complex in what was the original heritage area of Vancouver, Gastown on Water Street. Designed by Richard Henriquez, architect, Gastown Square was completed in 1974. The footprint plan, **120,** shows the hollow public space wrapped around by this building. The outline building form is of a horseshoe, a lucky horseshoe in fact. Four storeys high, with a street frontage barely more than fifty-one paces, the building while not large is profoundly recognizable on the street.

Buildings do not have to be large to be good architecture, as Gastown Square attests. Regretfully, one of the fall outs in these fulsome days of power and money is that we have failed to make a distinction between big architecture and good architecture. We have fallen for the erroneous dictum: bigger is best. Indeed, the profession's preoccupation with procuring prestigious, important commissions has obscured their vision to the fact that a commission only becomes important when the participating people make it so. Size, budget, prestigious clients have never been a prerequisite for good architecture, and never will be.

Good urban architecture, as I have suggested, complements the urban space around itself and contributes to that space. It respects the neighbours, reflecting their time and their architectural details. Gastown Square fulfils these requirements admirably.

The area in Vancouver called Gastown is on the original townsite from which the modern city grew. As the warehousing centre servicing the region, the first substantial development began in the 1890s. Large masonry and timber structures were built. A flurry of development activity in the 1900s completed the area with one or two buildings going up in the 1930s. Originally the warehousing centre for the region, in the late sixties a new use had to be found and it became the first heritage area in the city.

The warehouses are of the old masonry and timber, post-and-beam floors and masonry-bearing wall construction. They enclose vast areas inside, principally designed for bulk storage. Consequently, because much of the interior is inaccessible to window light and ventilation, the space inside is not easily converted to contemporary uses. In fact, many of the buildings are large single-use, retail warehouse types, not quite in keeping with the new conception of what Gastown is supposed to be: namely, small varied spaces for artists, craftsmen and mixed retail uses with some offices. In some other traditional cities, such as St. John's and Victoria, the masonry warehouses were built smaller and they were built with a horseshoe type of layout, in contrast to the old buildings of Gastown but similar to Gastown Square. The horseshoe layout, no doubt, used in earlier times for off-street horse and cart delivery, makes for very easy conversion to contemporary use.

Gastown Square was designed by reflection in a horseshoe retail and office building layout compatible with the reuse of the area. And by responding to reality rather than convention, what could have been a dead-space interior became the creative inner spaces of the horseshoe layout. Indeed, Gastown Square's major strong point is the inside courtyard that is so much of a surprise when wandering in off the street.

The courtyard is a design principle that addresses the desirability for a passive ambience within an active, noisy city environment. With city traffic noises well above acceptable levels (appendices I and II), not only in Vancouver, but also in every city across the country, horseshoe space becomes virtually mandatory.

The footprint plan, **120,** does not adequately show how the courtyard of Gastown Square winds around the interior. Much of the courtyard space projects under the wraparound wings behind the main building, not visible on the footprint. Two entrances penetrate to the square from the street. One entrance is evident in the illustration, the other is covered by the four-storey front. The evident entrance is arched over by a slender foot bridge connecting the second floor of the main wing to the narrow portion of the complex running north and south. The other entrance is on the opposite side, winding under the solid form, running right into the under space of the back wings, making a retail mall half-covered, half-exposed to the sky. The back wings are lower than the street wing so as not to obscure a northern vista from the upper floor offices. The main form accommodating offices is sloped behind with a glass skylight. The sloping skylight allows sun to shine into the Square for much of the day winter and summer.

Gastown Square's most significant architectural attribute is on the street, the facade. The sensitive way it has been integrated into the line up of existing buildings is an attribute shared by all the neighbours. Looking at the facade from the east on the street, **121,** there is hardly a break from heritage building to new building. The new building, completed in 1974, is as one with its neighbours which were built at the turn of the century.

169

Figure 121. Gastown Square Water St. Vancouver B.C.

Gastown Square is contemporary architecture, make no mistake about that. The dark, burnt-masonry facing, coloured in variations of red violet to bright orange, melds into the traditional masonry of the neighbouring buildings. The chiaroscuro of the six bay windows on the front is abruptly different from the fenestration of the neighbours. Yet, the vertical bay window forms rhyme subtly with the vertical windows of the building, of the same height, down the street. As contemporary architecture, it fits well with traditional neighbours. Yet, the architectural design is not an obsequious reiteration of old details to appease the historical zealots. In an unassuming way, this is a bold use of contemporary materials and architectural forms. It slips into the street as though it has been there for as long as the other buildings. And that is the key to good urban architecture. No preponderance of obtrusive ego; with good design that is not needed. The quality of the architecture stands needless of overt demonstration.

170

The new St. Lawrence Neighbourhood in Toronto, **122,** has also slipped into the traditional street pattern with ease. Actually, ease is hardly the word for the project which was the subject of heated debate at the time of its inception. But considering the magnitude of the development and the energy expended on the construction, amazingly, it has become a tacitly accepted part of the community now. We can easily sit back to admire the achievement.

St. Lawrence Neighbourhood is the newly constructed area bounded to the south by the railway lines, to the north of

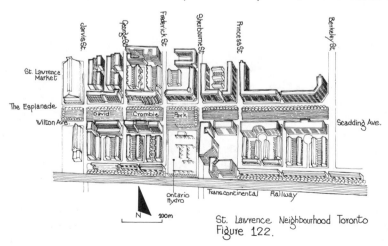

St. Lawrence Neighbourhood Toronto
Figure 122.

The Esplanade, jutting further north between Jarvis and Sherbourne to Front Street, and stopped east and west respectively by Parliament and Yonge Streets. It is a lot of city. Completed in the early 1980s and still going on, it is a newly conceived residential community right in the heart of Toronto, replacing old industrial land, parking lots, vehicle storage lots and all the old stuff coming out of the refuse of the industrial city. What a relief it is!

The Esplanade, the significant urban space between Berkeley and Market Streets, is the main focus of St. Lawrence. Formed as a *grande allée*, in fact it is a park, more of a passive urban green space than a moving, marching, *allée.*

Grande allée images are a left over from the regal days of the imperial city, evoking images of boulevards with double rows of trees following the length of the pavement. There is no place for such images in the contemporary city. Nowhere can such a swath of land be naturally placed. Double lines of trees is a platitude looking good in drawings, satisfying to the renderer, but of little spatial impact when installed. There is something pathetically reminiscent of failed royalists lurching for grandeur about trees planted like soldiers waiting to be shot. Trees provide shade and there is something to be said for shade trees in David Crombie Park. However, boulevard trees lined up alongside a thoroughfare do not help pedestrians who are trying to avoid the noise of traffic. For the sake of reposeful urban space, trees are better used when they are clustered around a protected space. A protected space where parents and children can relax out of the blazing sun.

Enclosure along the perimeter of The Esplanade space by the surfaces of the surrounding buildings is more the conclusive feature, the double row of trees is hardly noticeable. Enclosing facades fortuitously follow the street alignment. Behind the high facades are horseshoe wraparound spaces enclosing and shielding two-storey residential buildings from noise and street activity. The facades are masonry. The colour of the masonry from facade to facade is compatible, ranging from bright magenta to purple.

The transcontinental railway runs by on the southern perimeter of St. Lawrence neighbourhood. How can the quiet of a residential neighbourhood be preserved alongside the noise of speeding transcontinental trains? Can the noise be entirely blocked out? Disturbing levels of noise can be ameliorated, abated by placing solid forms of buildings between the source

171

of noise, creating reposeful positive spaces. This is how the noise has been shielded in St. Lawrence. Along the railway tracks, buildings have been placed to shield the public open space from the railway noise. The strategy is known as placing buffer buildings. For the public urban space of the St. Lawrence Neighbourhood, it has been successful. For the private spaces along the track, it has not been so effective.

Buildings make good sound shields. By making the buildings into buffers of noise small space microclimates have been created inside the horseshoe spaces behind the buffers. Quiet there is evident. How the same thing works for the residents in the buffer buildings is another matter. Double glazing and sound insulation is a dubious foil against the least of railway noise. Residential accommodation inside the apartments in those buffer buildings look towards the source of noise. No matter what the treatment of double glazing, etc., noise in those circumstances will prevail. The apartments would have been better designed with single-loaded corridors with the back of the corridor facing the noise, the living space of the apartment facing into the peaceful space.

Public urban space is formed by the buildings with which it is enclosed. The examples cited in this chapter all derive their most satisfying spatial attributes by following this dictum. The enclosing facades of the surrounding buildings can be designed to make the public urban space into an amenable microclimate, by protecting the space from traffic noise, by reflecting sunshine into the space and by protecting it from the prevailing winds. Also, it can be attractive to people by being designed in an inviting, easily accessible and convenient manner, a haven of harmonious circumstance. For public urban space is the city and St. Lawrence demonstrates that well.

172

8
Tending the City

Never in previous history have we had the resources to make such massive changes to our cities in so short a period of time. Haussmann's reconstructions of the Right Bank in Paris and Nash's realignment of Regent Street in the West End of London were large urban undertakings and their legacy is great beauty. Haussmann's concept was massive; nothing like it had been seen. The development of Paris was a spider's web effecting reconstruction on many streets simultaneously. The work in London, on one street, affected all the surrounding urban spaces.

For large-scale development, concentrated on one inner city site, Paris and London do not match up to the St. Lawrence Neighbourhood. In London and Paris, at the time, development was disruptive. The disruptive effects were the crucial elements in those cities. St. Lawrence Neighbourhood was not disruptive for there were no previous residents to disturb. The site was uninhabited industrial land but the general effect spread far beyond the immediate area. Compared to Nash's and Haussmann's experience St. Lawrence was a mild intrusion.

Disruption or plain sailing in the next decades, our cities will go through redevelopments of varying magnitudes. Projects of a scale more extensive than those of Haussmann and Nash will have to be contemplated, if we are to heal the wounds inflicted on the modern city. For unpopular as redevelopment may be, the era of massive city rebuilding is just about to start. For some cities, nothing short of complete renewal will be able to make amends. Large-scale renewals, towers and large complexes with integrated local reconstructions, gardens and family spaces will be initiated. The millions currently spent on perfidious, promotional hype will be directed to serious planning. Ultimately, the complex, uneven, life-giving patina of the city will be addressed. Slogans such as small is beautiful, down with the bulldozer, etcetera, will be shelved. Get-rich-quick artists will be as pervasive as ever, no doubt, but it is hoped that government will not be imbued with their snake oil message. Considered, sensitive, realistic, creative thought will take their place. It will have to.

We will come to our senses. When we do, we will realize the city is a principle source of wealth. Wealth, not on paper, but wealth as a human resource, gainfully occupied producing useful goods, restructuring our living environment. Our irrational, emotional craving for easy money, instant gratification, will become rational, emotional seeking for a decent place to live and work. One day, we will confront our wasted efforts: making silly techno-war toys does not a wealthy people make.

Wealth is people working and recreating in close interaction. Only close interaction between people makes a city healthy and wealthy. When we awaken from our myopic sleep we will see the cultural opportunities, the economic opportunities, the job opportunities encompassed by the restoration of our cities. Until that impending day dawns, we will continue writing of ideals.

Some would say in futility, for the human species is indelibly cast in sorrow. And others have more faith—and I am one of them—so they write about sharing visions of urban space, imagining it, delineating broad principles of design, ideas long forgotten, awaiting renewed energies.

I try to see the city as more than a fast opportunity, although I do not discount such rewards. I see the city as an opportunity for the exercise of one of the most noble of human instincts: the art of creating living space. The city, simply put, is space. To reiterate, I see buildings as solid forms and spaces as positive forms, the interstices between solid forms.

The art of city building requires that we insert each building carefully into the city fabric so as to contribute a piece of space to the overall urban complexity. Public urban space is the city. It gives the city meaning. This is where we start tending the city.

Of necessity, there are various levels upon which the city may be tended, like tending a garden. Everyone knows how to tend a garden. They pay attention to it. They care for it. They

174

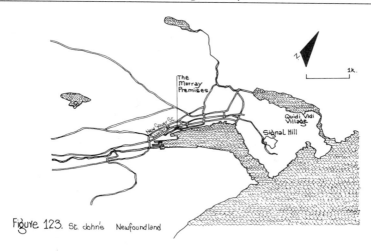

Figure 123. St. John's Newfoundland

175

plant in season, hoe, weed, thin out, fertilize and eventually enjoy the blooms and fragrance. They take from the garden only what they give. This is how the urban environment should be tended too.

Tending the city starts by looking at what is there. Some cities are fortunate to have a good start. Small scale thinning and replanting will suffice, like the lucky horse shoe cities, St. John's and Victoria. In such small centres, old buildings and street layouts are still very much in use.

St. John's on the Atlantic Coast, figure **123,** is one such place where the historic fabric of the city directs the present-day development. A city where the inevitable topography— the slope to the harbour—took over and keeps a strong hold today. Downtown St. John's, **124,** is small but it has a lot to say about city design.

St. John's, together with Victoria on the Pacific Coast, is a lucky horseshoe city because so many buildings and public urban spaces replicate the form of a horseshoe: open to the street, the inner space is surrounded by building. Inside open space then becomes a useful courtyard, protected from the noisy traffic on the street.

Because it is a small historic city St. John's comprises many small masonry warehouses, lucky horseshoes. The buildings were built, for various reasons, with a hollow court-yard middle. The street alignment is almost always followed and the steep slope of the hill away from the harbour dictates a linear regular pattern. Coarse grain traffic, trucks and cars, run along streets that follow the contours. Pedestrians climb

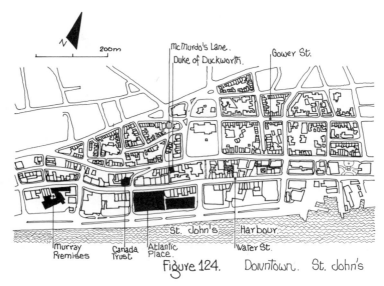

Figure 124. Downtown. St. John's

the steps across them. Small buildings add up, by increments, to the ensuing urban spaces. St. John's is an excellent place to explain the finer points of tending the garden of the city.

The Murray Premises, **125,** in downtown St. John's is a perfect example of a lucky horseshoe design that came from an old waterfront warehouse. The architectural preservation

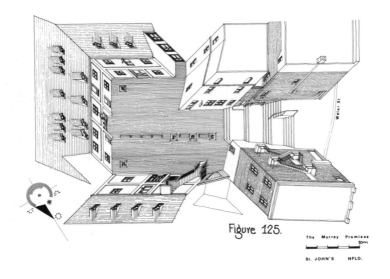

Figure 125.

The Murray Premises
St. JOHN'S   NFLD.

Entrance to
Murray Premises

Water Street
St. John's Nfld.

Figure 126.

177

design work was carried out by Beaton Sheppard, architect.
These buildings had been in use as commercial dockside
buildings since the fire of 1846. The inner courtyard connects
to Water Street by way of a corridor-like passage opening into
the horseshoe. The passage is a surprise. Walking along
Water Street, just past Tooton's, the unsuspecting pedestrian
could easily walk right past. But if they are sharp, Murray
Premises open up just beyond the stepped passage.

Water Street, the main street of downtown St. John's,
126, is developing rapidly by accretion. New buildings fit into
the old streetscapes, without upheaval. Most of the new buildings seem always to fit politely rather than to disrupt. In scale
and appearance they just add to the small spaces and street
alignments. The Canada Trust Building on Beck's Hill, by
Charles Cullum and Beaton Sheppard, architects, and the
Central Trust, on Water Street, meld into the streetscape.

There is one sad recent addition that infringes on the island's neighbourly politeness. Intruding, imposing the modern habits from "aways", is a bank tower on Water Street at
Beck's Cove. The tower, just another glass thing sporting the
usual amorphous street plaza, has no place in St. John's. The
plaza does nothing to provide a pedestrian pause; such spatial
adjuncts never do. But a continuous street alignment is dis-

turbed and the visual effect of traditional materials on the street has been disrupted. The original scale is jeopardized. As of 1987, this is the first intrusion of its kind on Water Street; let's hope it is the last. Even the large shopping centre, Atlantic Place, respected (by its masonry facade) the flow of the street.

St. John's is a city in which development by accretion is still appropriate. Staying within tradition, a patchwork layout ensures scale, appearance and continuity of a shared vision of space attained by habit, tradition and the compelling to- pography of the harbour and the sloping site. The shared vi- sion is incremental in approach, building by building, space by space.

178

That approach is fine for a small, traditional city. Howev- er, incremental shared visions are not the way Western society builds in the dynamic centres of power. Sentiment and nostal- gia has a place in the thrust of the modern city, but it seems relegated to personal preference rather than to planned vi- sions. Still, incremental development need not be either sen- timental or nostalgic. In fact, incremental planning can, and should, be integrated into high-density developments, high- rise towers and modern systems to make the city more effi- cient and reliable. Pros and cons of high-rise development is polarized; finer points are lost in the intense debate. Never- theless, modern society, technology and the livable city are not aways incompatible.

Time and time again protest groups formulate their ar- guments against high-rise and density without considering the realistic implications of what may be done instead. De- spite the image of intense urbanization, Canada is still a cul- ture firmly rooted in an agricultural past. Many groups seem to think the ideal city is a greenspace park, pristine and lush on the inside with us looking in from the perimeter, on the outside. They bolster their argument by declaring low- rise can accommodate the same density as high-rise by re- designing the block layout.

There is a sometime quoted theory by Sir Leslie Martin, delivered in a lecture at Harvard in 1966, on the subject of high-rise versus low-rise. He conjectured that a few blocks in Manhattan, including the Union Carbide tower and Rocke- feller Centre, averaging twenty stories in height, could be reduced to seven stories by building over the cross streets and deploying seven-storey courtyard buildings around successive open spaces. Why a seven-storey building is more pleasant in which to live is not explained. But of course his point was to demonstrate the redundancy of tower buildings. His theory is immaculate, to be sure, but difficult to apply. Sir Leslie addresses the unrealistic notion that the cross streets can be included in density computations on privately owned sites, or even that the cross streets can be built over at all. The developer in the city now has to contend with the area of the site he owns, the price he paid and the ticking clock of the interest rates he'll ultimately have to borrow on. The argument will never be settled conclusively, for each side devises its own criteria. But a simple experiment on a downtown block in Edmonton, **127**, applying Sir Leslie's theory demonstrates its limitations.

179

The typical block has a developed ratio of floor space to ground area (FSR) of just over six. This is not an unusual figure considering that in Montreal on Dominion Square the ratio is twenty-one. The developer cannot include the streets in his calculations. Current requirements allow him to consider only the ratio between what he wants to build and the area of the site he has just paid cash for. The overall ratio including streets and open spaces is not much help to him, unless of course he is prepared to use his project for a protracted and expensive test case to challenge the system.

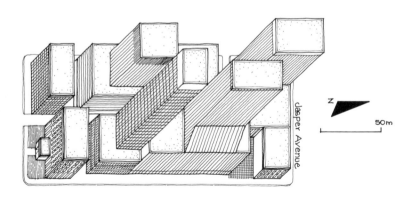

Volume	523,000m³	Typical Block Development
Area	180,000m²	Edmonton.
Site	24,000m²	
F.A.R.	7.5 Max. 27 storeys	Figure 127.

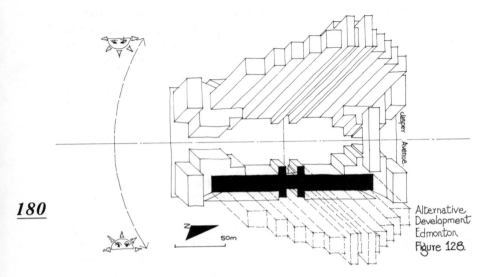

180

Alternative
Development
Edmonton
Figure 128.

Let's apply a lucky horseshoe space and the related street alignments to an imaginary development on the block. The towers in our construction do not block the inside space from sunlight and they do not loom imminently over the street. Ratio of floor space to ground area is the same as for the buildings shown in **127**. Heights are kept as low as possible. The resulting development is shown in **128**. Heights remain pretty much the same; site coverage is better because of the inside open space and the facades on the street are marginally lower and of a uniform height (although I'm not sure that is an attribute).

Edmonton is one of those winter cities where civic minded people are looking for ways to make downtown usable all year round. And those people may see the lucky horse shoe open space as contrary to their concepts. Indeed, there are plans afoot to enclose most of the downtown at some time, something like a grand West Edmonton mall. Hopefully, a more sensitive approach to the winter city will ultimately prevail. For, if a large part were to be enclosed, much of its impact would be lost in the incessant plastic glitter that comes from that type of development. Surely there are better ways to treat the winter city. Thoreau wrote, "Winter is not an evil to be abolished but a subject worthy of the true artist". Does his point of view have any currency in the winter urban milieu of today?

On a more mundane level, the floor to site area ratio of six could result in an uninteresting building covering the whole site of six stories high. But is low-rise the only criterion? Surely not. Somehow a low box does not seem to be a desirable alternative, for it would be no more than a chunk of covered built up area. Can we conclude from this that high-rise in the urban centre is not only inevitable but with special design could be an amenity? Obviously, when so many other factors are brought to bear, we cannot allow urban design to bog down in such a sterile argument forever. The sooner tower building forms are accepted for what they are—the sooner integrated—various, beautiful urban spaces will be a part of the city.

Ideally, a city should be made up of all forms of building types: high, low, lucky horseshoes, even some chaos with some relief. And there are some cities that are going that way. Victoria has a part of the downtown area that is almost entirely horseshoe buildings. New development is taking place—commercial towers and malls—close to the lucky horseshoe area that is sacrosanct.

181

The horseshoe area in Victoria, **129,** is in the part of downtown built during the last century. It is replete with old brick warehouse buildings, horseshoe spaces, open to the sky. Once they were used as marine storage buildings close to the docks and transportation facilities. The area changed in the 1980s and is now a main tourist attraction, in the central part of the downtown. A part of it includes Chinatown; most of it

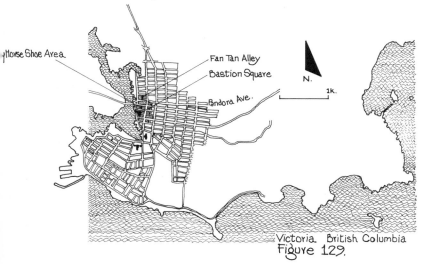

Victoria British Columbia
Figure 129.

is reconstructed into shopping malls, restaurants and entertainment areas.

A few blocks, **130,** of the lucky horseshoe area demonstrates the way the old buildings, with fortuitously open inner spaces, have been linked into a comprehensive pedestrian system that connects up across the whole of downtown Victoria. Most of the horseshoe buildings are redeveloped around three main spaces: Market Square, a commercial retail building; Waddington Alley, a retail pedestrian way; and Bastion Square. The latter is an old heritage public open space surrounded by reconstructed heritage buildings. All these spaces connect to Chinatown, the street running one block to the north, through Fan Tan Alley.

New buildings occur occasionally throughout the area. A large parking garage of 1960s vintage, backing onto Bastion Square, is the most voluminous. Figure **130,** displays the potential interplay between positive spaces and solid building forms. Variety of pedestrian spaces, the irregularity of the shapes, the opportunities for small views and longer vistas is limitless. Such a complexity of unexpected spaces affords a satisfying experience so often missed in modern developments. Bastion Square, **131,** rounds out the concept and is a most satisfying urban space.

Free-standing buildings punctuate the space of Bastion Square. This is a rare spatial form. Once a through street, Bastion Square was blocked from connecting to Wharfe Street and made over into a reposeful urban space. The large free-

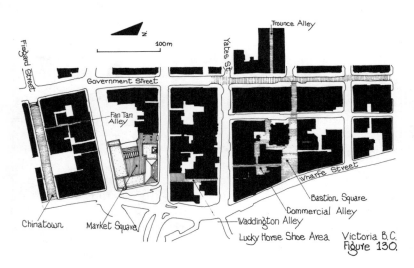

Victoria, B.C.
Figure 130.

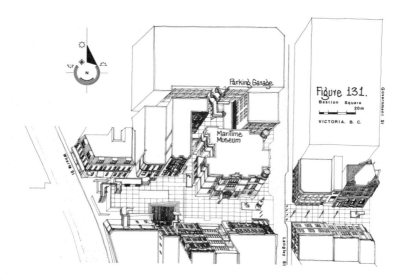

Figure 131.
Bastion Square
20m
VICTORIA. B. C.

183

standing building with the two domes was Victoria Court House and has since become the Maritime Museum.

Buildings in the lucky horseshoe area have all been redeveloped as increments of the overall design, including Bastion Square. The shared vision of urban space, developed piece by piece, some small, some a bit larger, and the circulation in connecting links, seems to come out of habitual necessity.

Often as not, space in most cities is a matter of a bit of paving, a bit of landscaping and buildings designed and constructed oblivious to their role as components of the image of the city. But cultivating the city goes far beyond a bit of paving and landscaping. And, until cultivating the city becomes recognized as comprehensive policy, not much will improve. Paving, landscaping palliatives consume too much civic resource compared to their weak effect.

No point in complaining, however. Rather lay out some principles to show a better way of seeing the city. New principles involve risks and without a quantum shift in general values they remain dormant. But, if we do not persist: postulating, changing and improving, making attempts, keeping ideas flowing, the old banal chaos will keep on rolling along.

The following are some basic ground rules. They are minimal, giving architects and planners the chance to do what they have been trained to do properly; design buildings and spaces, not wrestle with regulations. Extensive, complicated rules don't work; witness what we see before us now. Evidence in many cities shows multiple planning hoops have negligible effect. Some cities have virtually no rules; some have volumes. In either case, the downtowns are indistinguishable: the same glass hulks sitting there isolated, the same ad hoc fractionated urban spaces, the same din. Rules or no rules we are consumed by the destructive imperative of modern business. Rules without a vision have no effect. A vision without means of implementation has even less effect.

The following requirements are founded on an imagined shared vision of urban space. The vision combines the attributes of sensitively integrated towers and lucky horseshoe urban areas and is implemented by requirements that touch on principles rather than rigid rules.

In a multicultural society such as Canada, the idea of a shared vision may fly in the face of diversity. We are a country hospitable to many cultures. Can such a mix countenance a vision of the city that betokens the melting pot? The answer is yes, because a shared vision is not to be adopted so rigorously as to exclude cultural variety and diversity.

A shared vision of urban space is a modest principle for it applies in this context to urban design and then only on a street by street, neighbourhood by neighbourhood, place by place, basis. The protagonists sharing the vision have a broad inclusive sense of space. Hopefully, that sense will be enriched and diversified by cultural differences.

A way of imagining space must be understood by all members of the design and planning team. The present process of design development—a cross between number crunching, mind-numbing infighting to save a bit of creativity, and mind-boggling, *laissez-faire*, no-holds-barred chaos—must be replaced with a reasonably sensitive approach. All the protagonists must first agree that their individual best interests are served by co-operation and that in itself may be a tall order.

The six requirements forming the basis of the shared vision go like this—and remember the purpose of an urban design requirement is not to keep city hall busy but to guide a series of developments to result in our shared set of urban standards—simple, to the point and enforceable.

1. **Interim Land Use.** This is a requirement that protects the shared vision from the temptation to succumb to expedient *ad hoc* piecemeal opportunities. Large develop-

ments take decades to complete. Cities are replete with underused and unused small sites languishing as parking lots, empty spaces, holes in the ground, etcetera. Time limits set unrealistic development schedules on very large projects that may lie fallow for twenty years or more. Expedient *ad hoc* development may usurp the agreed upon process before the major land use plan can be completed. Interim land use requires that the land be put to use temporarily for aesthetic or utilitarian purposes: planting, seeding, park, whatever, instead of remaining as an eyesore or a detriment to the community, often as a carpark or a dump.

2. **Site Development.** This requirement phases construction according to need. Large scale planned developments, in which the initial promotion presentations are realized according to their original promise, are rare. Architectural promotional presentations evoking unrealistic expectations ultimately encourage public cynicism. Accordingly, site development plans should be conceptual and in skeletal form. Site development plans should enunciate goals on a small neighbourhood by neighbourhood, area by area basis. Phasing emphasizes small manageable increments.

185

3. **Environment.** Two conceptual requirements underlie environmental planning.

i. *Pollution.* Nuisance, toxic waste above and below ground, noxious odour, excessive noise, visual blight, activity contrary to accepted use and occupancy and disturbance to peace are excluded.

ii. *Microclimates.* Public urban space and site planning should be designed to take advantage of the surrounding environmental attributes. The shape and solid forms of buildings should be moulded, spaced, and clad to create microclimate environments. Buildings should be designed to shield public and private open space from noise, traffic and overlooking views.

4. **Architectural form.** This signifies that buildings are to be shaped and articulated to create public urban space. "Form follows function" should be interpreted to mean that the outer shape of the building follow the function of the public urban space as well as its inner workings.

Public space is identified by place and need. Parks, plazas, squares, courtyards, boulevards, streets and lanes, shorelines, burial grounds, river valleys and ravines are all elements considered necessary to make a beautiful viable inner city.

They should define space pauses, entrance needs and traffic movement into an integrated fabric of urban reality.

Separate building facades should be designed to accumulate the effect of public urban space. Neighbouring facades should aggregate to more than a sum of each part. A co-ordinating device facilitating the accumulation should be instigated as a guiding framework. Individual buildings, accumulating over the life of the development, should be guided by the device to follow the collectively-agreed-to urban vision, buffer the noise from traffic and define microclimates. Such a device, the IBEX, is decribed later.

The architectural characteristics under the headings *Plastique* and *Palette* described in the list of "The Elements of Urban Space" (chapter four), should be taken into account.

5. **Use and Occupancy.** Close convenient connection between work and living should be the guiding requirement of occupancy. Use and occupancy should respond to new types of modern manufacturing techniques. Cottage type industries should be allowed, limited only by civic, environmental and nuisance requirements. Work opportunity should be close to place of residence. Residence should be diversified and affordable to all segments of society. Small-scale work activity areas, manufacturing (all kinds of things from the rag trade to furniture), arts, crafts, educational, assembly, performance, communal facilities, as well as retail stores and offices, should be integrated within dense residential areas.

6. **Movement.** Movement should be plotted to reflect realistically the use of the space. Separation of traffic should be accorded low priority. A coarse-grain mix, pedestrian, bicycle, slow moving vehicular traffic should be encouraged to hamper the use of high velocity, intense movement.

Fine-grain, single-type movement should be confined to pedestrian use only in the downtown spaces. And where possible single-use pedestrian traffic should be the norm in the downtown. High velocity, fine-grain, single-use traffic movement should be relegated to peripheral areas.

That concludes the six development requirements. They are evoked immediately below in three circumstances, in three separate Canadian cities that I have chosen to demonstrate their applications.

The first living example is place d'Youville in Quebec City.

The Province of Québec enjoys a unique cultural distinc-

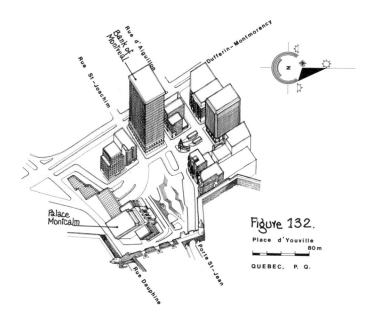

Figure 132.

Place d'Youville
80 m

QUEBEC, P. Q.

tion. The arts, particularly film, literature and theatre have an energy rarely found on the North American continent. Québec has a concentrated French-speaking people, an indigenous music and many other cultural characteristics that are distinctive. Ironically that distinction is not evident in architecture. Architecture in the province is as impervious to an autochthonous modern building form as anywhere else in Canada. Québec has its share of mindless modern hulks, *haute-vulgarité,* and place d'Youville is no exception.

Place d'Youville, **132,** is the regional transit centre of Quebec City. Just outside the walls of the old city, it lies alongside the commuter artery, Dufferin-Montmorency. Palais Montcalm is the dominant building, albeit not the largest. Walls enclose the eastern limits of the space as textured masonry and turreted portes. In stark contrast, the north and west, **133,** are festooned with high-rises designed oblivious to the qualities of whatever earlier buildings they have replaced.

My vision of urban space for place d'Youville, describes a new building that winds around the existing buildings, overpasses streets and completes the enclosure of place d'Youville on the west side. The enclosing facade brings together the broken-up appearance of the space. It masks the separate buildings, unifying the composition.

Place d'Youville, Before
Figure 133.

In accordance with requirement four (architectural form), a device to guide the development over a sustained time lapse is prescribed. Called an Imaginary Building Envelope, IBEX for short, (an IBEX is an urban design tool to help organize the line up of facades and building envelopes surrounding the public urban space) outlines a prospective building that will be built, **134.** It encourages development by increments, purposely. Various stages of building may be completed at any time, so long as the basic form and facade is maintained.

The acronym IBEX shares the name, appropriately, with a handsome, fleet-of-foot mountain goat, describes a framework-like set of imaginary lines that determine the shape and volume of buildings and prescribes the outline of their facades to enclose the west side of place d'Youville.

The IBEX derives from a similar urban design tool invented in New York. There it is called a build-to line. The

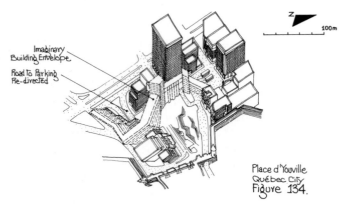

Imaginary
Building Envelope

Road to Parking
Re-directed

z
100m

Place d'Youville
Québec City
Figure 134.

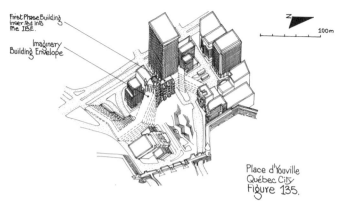

First Phase Building
inserted into
the IBE.

Imaginary
Building Envelope

100m

Place d'Youville
Québec City
Figure 135.

build-to line is a plane set at the street front up to which the building must be built. It is less effective than the IBEX. It is used to ensure continuous street alignments and to preserve views. The exclusive purpose of the IBEX is to coordinate the separate acts of design and development, over an indeterminate time frame, to bring about an enclosed space that fulfils the shared vision. It is a design tool devised to replace the current by-laws of thou shalt nots with a means of encouraging designers to work together. It should compel architects to project beyond the narrow concern of their immediate contracts.

In the course of building large developments downtown, progress can be capricious. The IBEX directs the separate building projects, completed by different organizations in different time slots, toward a stated goal. Its purpose is to mitigate the effects of capriciousness. On place d'Youville the first building to go in is shown in **135** and the complete concept is

189

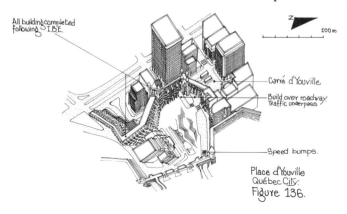

All buildings completed
following I.B.E.

100m

Carré d'Youville.

Build over roadway
Traffic underpass

Speed bumps.

Place d'Youville
Québec City.
Figure 136.

Place d'Youville, After.
Figure 137.

190   shown in **136.** There is no limit to the number of phases nor the time taken to develop the completed space, so long as the essential principles of the IBEX are followed.

Contrast appearance before development, **133,** with how the completed work looks in **137.**

The vision of space for place d'Youville has made a big change in traffic circulation. The bus circulation centre, in carré d'Youville, is visually separated from the formal space of place d'Youville. The gaping parking opening beside Palais Montcalm is masked by a building reflecting the appealing aspects of the old city. Parking remains accessible beneath. Architectural details of the new buildings, the turrets etc., rhyme with the icon of the Chateau Frontenac architecture. A narrow passage-like street, behind the new building, emulates the narrow streets so popular in the old city, i.e. ruelle des Ursulines.

From a made over, amorphous, urban circulation centre, place d'Youville is transformed into a public urban space. The image of place d'Youville is revived, for it can now be recognized as a gateway to and from the old city.

Downtown Saskatoon presents a challenge of a different nature. There is no spatial centre in the downtown other than Transit Terminus and the lawn in front of City Hall. Neither of these have been treated in a demonstrative way to suggest they are significant to the identity of the city.

No evidence suggests the city has succumbed to a tedious tourist boutique syndrome either. Nevertheless, for busy, active, well-used streets throughout the day and into the late evening the centre of Saskatoon is remarkable. For, although small, the city is the centre of agriculture, business and indus-

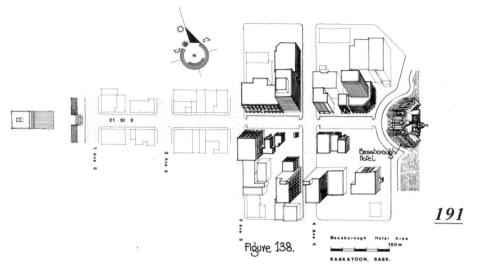

Figure 138.

Bessborough Hotel Area
100 m

SASKATOON, SASK.

191

try for a very large surrounding area. No surprise, then, that the downtown thrives.

Cultivating a public urban space in Saskatoon seems, therefore, to be appropriate. I have selected here an area nominally, on the periphery of the thriving centre: the four blocks, **138,** in front of the Bessborough Hotel. Some wide gaps show up and some potential heritage buildings are dotted around (as of 1987). Is it a good area in which to leave well enough alone? Don't worry, it's only an idea. And, in any case, if our senses inform us correctly, this area is imminent for redevelopment. Who knows, some good may come of our ruminations.

A vision of urban space for Saskatoon should be quite different from the one describing place d'Youville. The latter concerns the completion of an existing space with a continuous building form. Saskatoon requires an approach that allows for incremental, free-standing buildings to define a series of pedestrian spaces and walkways that can connect to the existing downtown.

Local conditions conspire against a repeat of place d'Youville. Instead, new buildings should be small, in keeping with what is already there. New spaces should connect in a variation of a lucky horseshoe spatial layout to existing streets and pathways. Small, incremental, free-standing, solid building forms inserted in between the existing buildings should wrap around and enclose numerous small spaces.

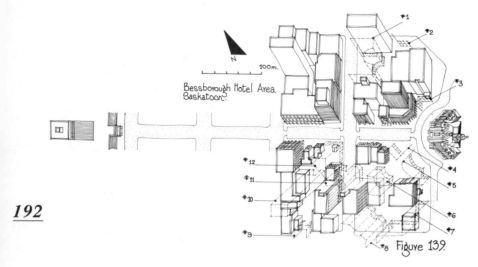

Figure 139.

192

Twelve separate buildings are described by twelve free-standing IBEX's, one for each building, **139.** Buildings are designed as three-dimensional sculptured forms. Facades are exposed to the public urban spaces in between. Potentially they may be used to show store fronts, entrances or windows.

The urban spaces build up over time; buildings are constructed by separate developers. The vision of urban space accumulates and is enhanced by each new building addition.

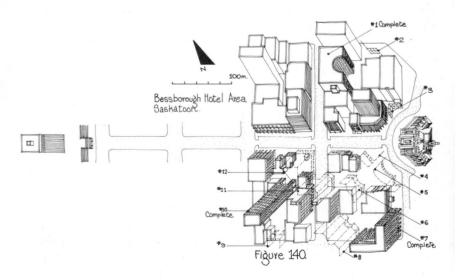

Figure 140.

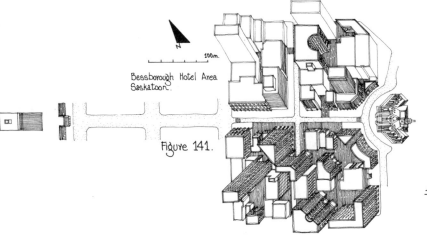

Bessborough Hotel Area
Saskatoon.

Figure 141.

193

Half completed, the development looks something like illustration **140**. Ultimately, the vision of urban space, when completed, follows the scale and appearance of the general development in the contiguous area, like **141**.

The principles of "The Elements of Urban Space", when used in conjunction with the IBEX, make following architectural trends unnecessary. The arcane world of current architecture contributes nothing to local public urban space because it is concentrated on styles and trends. Photographs of keystone arches, constructivism, deconstructivism, columnated attics are okay to sell stylish internationals. But it has nothing to do with public urban space and the details of design should be subsumed in favour of the impact of the composed, collected facades on it.

Within that framework, the rhyme of local architectural heritage (except that we have to be careful not to smother contemporary creativity) and the list of "The Elements of Urban Space" ought to be the principal criteria upon which style is based. Within that context, the creativity of architect and planner need know no bounds.

The final scenario in which the requirements and principles are applied is in Winnipeg. A familiar genre, the project is one of a type that will be seen often as the future unfolds in many contemporary Canadian cities. The project is the development of the East Yards, old railway land.

Opening industrial land to new development and reconsidering the relationship that land has to the existing city is a recurring theme. A number of possible redevelopment projects are similar to Winnipeg's: Bassin Louise, basse ville de Québec, the rail yards in Regina, Coal Harbour in Vancouver, the Songhees land in Victoria and of course those already mentioned, Pacific Place, Vancouver and, in Toronto, Harbourfront.

The East Yards lands are fifty-two hectares (129 acres) of usable area. Currently the Canadian National Railway's marshaling yards occupy the land. As such their days are numbered. Contiguous to the downtown, bounded by the rivers and isolated by the rail line and a busy throughway from the city, the land is not unlike so many of the other inner city industrial reuse projects. So far, no extensive architectural development initiatives have been accepted. An outline plan may, therefore, be appropriate.

Definitive detailed drawings of the architectural forms, describing how the land will be developed and used into a future extending some twenty years is a feat of prediction beyond reliable projection and imagination. Too often planning is confused with architecture. Many of the drawbacks associated with Harbourfront and Pacific Place are the result of applying architectural renderings to what is essentially a planning function.

Therefore I propose an alternative approach on the Winnipeg lands. Who knows what urban land requirements will be in twenty years? The last twenty years tells us such predictions are capricious. Accordingly, an outline framework of reference to guide the physical development along the six requirements only is postulated.

Interim land use. The land is still used for railway purposes. There is, therefore, a time of grace to cogitate. Make it into a park after the railway is no longer in use until a site development plan and definite development projects are in place.

Site development. I have enunciated some very simple goals for the site development plan. It is a broad physical layout to direct future phases describing the location of public urban spaces and buffer buildings only. From this simple layout a network of streets and secondary urban spaces, flotillas of necessary functions, will be generated in the future according to the needs of the future.

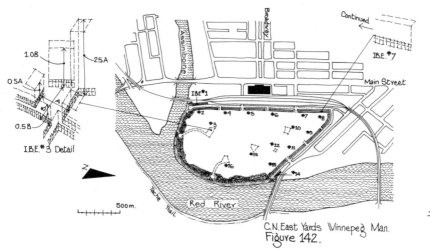

C.N. East Yards Winnepeg Man.
Figure 142.

195

The first goal of site development is to deal with the perimeter of the site. There are two categories of space and utility on the perimeter, the river banks and the roads and rail, that require different treatment.

First category. The river banks I have designated lineal parks. The park area, here, is depicted in scribble hatching. The first broad plan outline is shown in **142.**

Second category. On the landward side, the edges close to the road and railway, I have lined up buffer buildings (specially designed buildings, single-loaded corridors to protect the quiet residential public urban space from noise) to shelter residential and passive urban spaces. Buffer buildings are described in IBEX form in 11 separate buildings (IBEX #1, #2, #4, #5, #6, #7, #8, #9, #11, #13, #14). At the top right hand corner of the illustration a very rudimentary sketch shows the buffer IBEX. This IBEX is a simple outline, dotted line drawing that describes the envelopes of the proposed buildings.

The second goal of site development is to set out the overall development plan, **142,** and it comprises five outlined locations of public urban spaces only (in dotted outline, #3, #10, #12, #15 and #16). A rudimentary sketch to the left of **142** describes the IBEX for public urban space #3 and the volumetric envelope of the potential surrounding buildings. Proportions, height of buildings to width of space and outline of architectural details are prescribed. Proportions are shown in the sketch, for instance, as 2.5 of A. That specifies the height of the building in relation to the width of the public urban space at A (as described in chapter five). The IBEX describes the building facades as they will line up and form the public urban space at #3. It describes the building and spatial envelope overall and the architectural characteristics at street level.

The five public urban spaces described by the IBEXs are the crucial elements in the overall development plan. They set a concept of public urban space as the generator of the street layout. Development of roads, buildings and subsidiary public urban spaces will mesh around these spaces. They are the nodes of movement and interest that will encourage small spaces and streets to crop up, as and when necessary.

Subsequent development stages, on the Winnipeg lands, follow the other four requirements. As phasing progresses portions of the site are developed one at a time. The buildings may, after the first couple of phases, look like **143**. The park is completed and a walkway along the riverside park following the rivers reflects Taché Trail on the opposite side. Traffic turn-around circles connect to the main city street system. Buildings enclose the predetermined public urban spaces, #15 and #16. Two buffer buildings shade new street oriented buildings from traffic noise. Development proceeds following a set program, a shared vision, yet there is still room for contingent change of pace.

At this stage there are still three public urban spaces #3, #10 and #12, left to direct future development. Planning

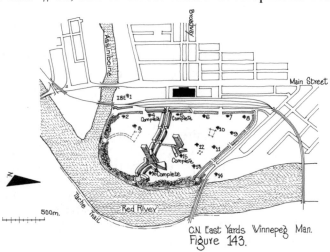

C.N. East Yards Winnepeg Man.
Figure 143.

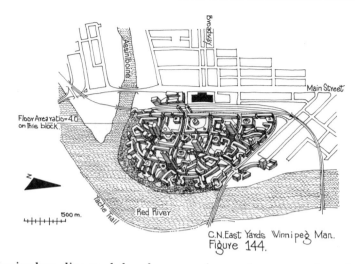

Floor Area ratio = 4.0 on this block

500 m.

N

C.N.East Yards Winnipeg, Man.
Figure 144.

priority has directed development by setting up nodes of spatial concentration. Everything else springs from that, as it is composed to enhance living and working conditions. Traffic has been relegated to a lesser priority.

The development is ultimately completed, **144.** Flexibility within the plan allows for future economic and cultural changes. Building forms reflect a vision that emphasizes priority of public urban space. Buildings and spaces form lucky horseshoes and towers. Densities are moderate: one block is proportionately developed to an FSR (Floor Space Ratio— divide the area of the building by the area of the site) of 4.5 times the ground area. Sir Leslie Martin's conjecture is fulfilled. Blocks comprise low, lucky horseshoes following the street alignments. Towers overlook and surround public urban spaces. Public open space is interwoven with private space. The idiosyncrasies of the people who use the buildings and spaces will add patina and texture way beyond immediate appearances. Diversity will come from all the requirements and principles discussed so far.

Throughout this book emphasis has been placed on public urban space as the heart of city design. The above overall development plan is all that is needed, so far as the requirements of urban design are concerned. I suggest it as an alternative to the customary, detailed architectural presentations that are usually proposed as overall development plans and are so unlikely to be implemented over decades of development.

Concluding a discussion on tending the city could appropriately hail the great challenges that lay ahead. A stimulating legacy has been bequeathed to the young and eager architects and planners. Eternally the optimists, faced with what we expected thirty years ago, can we still be sanguine? If we are, will our optimism be accompanied by hoots of we've heard it all before? In the late bloom of the twentieth century the phrase seems all too appropriate. Still, there remains a challenge to courage and imagination. Cities have always presented opportunity. How sadly we have failed to rise to the occasion. Indeed, how sad that with all our history, knowledge and power over nature we can think of nothing better to do in the cities than waste our efforts on trivialities. We can think up nothing more useful than shopping malls, phoney heritage tart-ups, overpriced condos replete in a deep sludge of vulgar luxury—and other places to waste our valuable resources.

198

We have long been profligate with the urban environment. We have created for ourselves a hostile, anxiety-ridden atmosphere. We defile our living and work space with din, stink and ugliness. We raid the wilderness for trivial glamour and thrills. We deny other living creatures a say in their survival. Our cities are a drain on the natural resource base. We give nothing in return. That will not last. The environment will strike back.

The city is a resource much like any other. It needs tending. The resource must be husbanded, farmed as though it were renewable, which indeed it is. What does this say of us? Each generation has the opportunity to express itself through the medium of the city. No doubt we will learn to cultivate and hoe. We will learn to harvest the crop with respect and judgement. We will learn to plant and thin, to cherish what has gone before, to discover the limits of our strengths and weaknesses. Indeed, we will learn the hard way. But, we will learn.

Appendix I

Noise Levels.

Noise levels have been taken with a hand held *Realistic* sound level meter, 'A' weighted network, at street level, during 1987-88. Some readings were taken in inside environments, in Jerry's Coffee Shop on Notre Dame, Montreal, for instance, to give a datum with which to make judgements. These inside environments along with other unusual instances have been marked with asterisks; other unusual instances refer to heavy truck traffic and outside rock music concerts. Readings were taken generally in areas of the Central Business Districts. Some exceptions were made, as for instance the By Ward Market in Ottawa. The exceptions are very close to the CBD's.

High noise levels are usually due to downtown construction activity, lunch-time concerts and heavy truck traffic. Civic lunch-time rock concerts are clearly very popular, as well as being of very high noise levels up to 80-101 decibels: Ottawa's Metcalfe @ Wellington plaza for instance. Trucks changing gear, moving from a stationary position increase the readings significantly. All these high noise levels are exacerbated by the sound box effect of space enclosures, hard surfaces of buildings, roads etc. situated to amplify sound reverberations. Abrupt wind gusts affect the readings significantly and have not been recorded.

One standard of exterior noise level exists in the National Building Code (1977). The code requires no more than 55 decibels be transmitted into an exterior, urban residential environment. A decibel is a unit used to measure and compare the intensity of sound.

CANADA.

VANCOUVER, B. C.
September 1987.
1). VAG steps.   82-6 decibels   1510 hrs. Wednesday.
2). Eaton's Plaza   76-82 decibels   1520 hrs. Wednesday.

3). Victory Square, centre	74-9 decibels	1400 hrs. Wednesday.
4). Hastings @ Cambie	84-92 decibels	1410 hrs. Wednesday.
5). Cambie Br. Smythe @ Beatty	80-2 decibels	1545 hrs. Wednesday.
6). Granville Mall @ Robson	76-88 decibels	1530 hrs. Wednesday.
7). Pigeon Park	84-9 decibels	1345 hrs. Wednesday.
8). Burrard Skytrain	76-8 decibels	1500 hrs. Wednesday.
9). Pacific Centre Mall Plaza	84-8 decibels	1630 hrs. Wednesday.
10). Cathedral Park, under glass	74-76 decibels	1430 hrs. Wednesday.
11). Dunsmuir @ Howe	90-94 decibels*	1435 hrs. Wednesday.
12). Royal Centre Lobby (inside)*	72-74 decibels	1700 hrs. Wednesday.
November 1988.		
13). Smithe @ Richards	68-74 decibels	1440 hrs. Tuesday.
14). Seymour @ Nelson	68-76 decibels	1500 hrs. Tuesday.
15). Helmken @ Seymour	72-79 decibels	1504 hrs. Tuesday.
16). Helmken @ Richards	66-78 decibels	1505 hrs. Tuesday.
17). Helmken @ Granville	66-76 decibels	1510 hrs. Tuesday.
18). Davie @ Granville	68-78 decibels	1515 hrs. Tuesday.
19). Davie @ Howe	68-81 decibels	1516 hrs. Tuesday.
20). Drake @ Howe	66-81 decibels	1520 hrs. Tuesday.
21). Drake @ Hornby	64-76 decibels	1525 hrs. Tuesday.
22). Anchor Point courtyard	64 decibels	1530 hrs. Tuesday.
23). Ventilator. @ Howe entrance	78 decibels steady	1531 hrs. Tuesday.
24). Hornby @ Pacific	76-84 decibels	1532 hrs. Tuesday.
25). Hornby @ Beach	66-72 decibels	1534 hrs. Tuesday.
26). Howe @ Beach	66-72 decibels	1535 hrs. Tuesday.
27). Howe St. end.	60-64 decibels	1538 hrs. Tuesday.
28). Alley behind Admiral	64-75 decibels	1538 hrs. Tuesday.
29). Under Granville Br. North	50 decibels	1540 hrs. Tuesday.
30). Inside Granville Market* Machine noise	64-66 decibels	1550 hrs. Tuesday.
31). Outside Info. Ctr. Gran. Isl.	62-66 decibels	1555 hrs. Tuesday.
32). Under Granville Br. South	68-75 decibels	1600 hrs. Tuesday.
33). Broadway @ Granville	74-82 decibels	1613 hrs. Tuesday.
34). 12th. Ave. @ Granville	74-86 decibels	1619 hrs. Tuesday.

CALGARY, Alta.
June 1987.

35). Olympic Plaza	64-72 decibels	0930 hrs. Wednesday.
36). Speaker's Corner	62-69 decibels	1030 hrs. Tuesday.
" "	64-73 decibels	1600 hrs. Tuesday.
37). City Hall Plaza	62-64 decibels	1530 hrs. Wednesday.
38). McDougall Centre East	62-66 decibels	1130 hrs. Wednesday.
39). " " West.	62-64 decibels	1030 hrs. Wednesday.

200

EDMONTON, Alta.
June 1987.

40). Jasper Ave. @ 103rd. Street	74-80 decibels	1730 hrs. Thursday.
41). Sir Winston Churchill Park	59-64 decibels	1830 hrs. Thursday.
42). City Hall Entrance Steps	64-66 decibels	1130 hrs. Thursday.
43). Rice-Howard Way	59-62 decibels	1600 hrs. Friday.

TORONTO, Ont.
August 1987.

44). Spadina Gardens	76-80 decibels	1600 hrs. Sunday.
45). Spadina @ Front	80-86 decibels	1200 hrs. Tuesday.
46). University Ave. @ Queens W.	84-92 decibels*	1415 hrs. Tuesday.
47). Market Square	72 decibels	1500 hrs. Saturday.
48). Nathan Phillips Sq. @ Archer	77-78 decibels	1200 hrs. Friday.
49). S.E. corner	82-84 decibels	1430 hrs. Friday.
,, ,,	76 decibels	1545 hrs. Tuesday.
50). David Crombie Park.	72-74 decibels	1045 hrs. Saturday.
51). Trinity Square.	79-80 decibels	1515 hrs. Friday.
52). Toronto-Dominion Centre	77-78 ecibels	1600 hrs. Tuesday.
53). Berczy Park	74 decibels	1630 hrs. Saturday.
54). @ Fountain	78-80 decibels	1015 hrs. Tuesday.
55). Larry Sifton Park	80 decibels	1600 hrs. Friday.
56). Clarence Square	72-76 decibels	1200 hrs. Tuesday.
57). 192 Sherbourne St. (inside)*	54-6 decibels	0730 hrs. Tuesday.
58). ,, ,,	64 decibel peaks as trucks pass	
59). Eaton's Galleria (inside)*	76 decibels	1630 hrs. Friday.
60). St. Lawrence Market (inside)*	82-83 decibels	1230 hrs. Saturday.
61). ,, ,, ,,	70-73 decibels	1415 hrs. Saturday.
62). Pier @ South end of Spadina	76-78 decibels	1145 hrs. Tuesday.
63). Harbour Front @ Power House	72-74 decibels	1115 hrs. Tuesday.
64). Yonge @ Front	84-90 decibels*	1000 hrs. Tuesday.

OTTAWA, Ont.
August 1987

65). Sparks Street Mall @ Lyon	78-84 decibels	1415 hrs. Monday.
66). ,, ,, ,, East end	74-80 decibels	1400 hrs. Monday.
67). Metcalfe/Wellington Plaza	76-82 decibels	0900 hrs. Monday.
68). ,, ,, ,,	79-81 decibels	1345 hrs. Monday.
69). ,, ,, ,,	98-101 decibels*	1215 hrs. Tuesday.
70). ,, ,, ,,	76-78 decibels	1415 hrs. Wednesday.
71). Confederation Square	76-78 decibels	1400 hrs. Monday.
72). Canlands	78-79 decibels	1330 hrs. Monday.
73). Bank of Canada Plaza	78-80 decibels	1550 hrs. Tuesday.
74). By Ward Market	76-78 decibels	1345 hrs. Wednesday.
75). Rideau Street	70-72 decibels	0600 hrs. Thursday.
	85-90 decibels*	0600 hrs. Thursday.

201

MONTREAL, P.Q.
August 1987.

76). Phillips Square	70 decibels	1600 hrs. Tuesday.
77). Dominion Square	64-72 decibels	1645 hrs. Tuesday.
78). Jerry's coffee shop (inside)*	74-78 decibels	1200 hrs. Thursday.
79). Place du Canada	66-74 decibels	1630 hrs. Tuesday.
80). Maison Alcan courtyard	59-62 decibels	1450 hrs. Wednesday.
81). Place D'Armes	62-84 decibels	1315 hrs. Tuesday.
82). Victoria Square	62-71 decibels	1000 hrs. Thursday.

QUEBEC CITY, P. Q.
August 1987.

83). Carré D'Youville	66-72 decibels	1130 hrs. Monday.

FREDERICTON, N. B.
August 1987.

84). Military Compound	66-72 decibels	1035 hrs. Wednesday.

SAINT JOHN, N. B.
August 1987.

85). North Market Wharf/ King St.	56 decibels	1210 hrs. Sunday.
86). King's Place	56-62 decibels	1130 hrs. Sunday.
87). City Hall Plaza	66-72 decibels	1503 hrs. Sunday.

MONCTON, N. B.
July 1987.

88). Assomption Plaza	58-62 decibels	1445 hrs. Thursday.
89). Oak Park	72 decibels	1200 hrs. Thursday.

CHARLOTTETOWN, P. E. I.
July 1987.
Confederation Centre for the Arts

90). On the street	62 decibels	1930 hrs. Tuesday.
91). Inside courtyard	52 decibels	1800 hrs. Tuesday.

HALIFAX, N. S.
July 1987.

92). Bedford Row	61-62 decibels	1030 hrs. Thursday.
93). Grand Parade	66-72 decibels	1500 hrs. Thursday.
94). Granville Mall	64-66 decibels	1030 hrs. Friday.
" "	86 decibels	1500 hrs. Saturday.

ST. JOHN'S, Newfld.
July 1987.

95). The Murray Premises	78-86 decibels	1230 hrs. Saturday.

UNITED STATES OF AMERICA.

WILLIAMSBURG, Virginia.
August 1988.

1). Boundary @ Jamestown Rd.	64-72 decibels	1500 hrs. Tuesday.
2). Duke of Gloucester @ S. Henry	58-62 decibels	1515 hrs. Tuesday.
3). Capital Building	50-52 decibels	1555 hrs. Tuesday.
4). Governor's Palace	56 decibels	1630 hrs. Tuesday.
5). Pulaski Club (1779 marker)	52 decibels	1707 hrs. Tuesday.

WASHINGTON, D.C.
September 1988.

6). Jefferson Monument	76 decibels	1600 hrs Friday.
7). " incoming jet over	80 decibels	1605 hrs. Friday.
8). Lincoln Memorial (aircraft over)	88-92 decibels*	1710 hrs. Friday.
9). SW 4th. @ NW Madison	76-84 decibels	1838 hrs. Friday.
10). Washington Mall @ SW C	69-74 decibels	1841 hrs. Friday.
11). SW 6th. @ SW C	76-82 decibels	1850 hrs. Friday.
12). SW 6th. @ SW C	76-86 decibels	0100 hrs. Saturday.
13). NW Constitution @ NW 12th.	81-83 decibels	1235 hrs. Saturday.
14). W entrance, E wing, Nat. Gallery	78-79 decibels	1432 hrs. Saturday.
15). Canadian Chancery, courtyard	76-79 decibels	1456 hrs. Saturday.
16). NW East @ NW 4th.	76-82 decibels	1513 hrs. Saturday.
17). Pennsylvania. Ave. @ NE 5th.	80-96 decibels*	1545 hrs. Saturday.
18). Union Station	72 decibels	0810 hrs. Sunday.

NEW YORK, N.Y.
September 1988.
Labour day.

19). W 53rd. St. @ 9th. Ave.	74-78 decibels	1040 hrs. Monday.
20). W 53rd. St. @ Broadway	78-84 decibels	1049 hrs. Monday.
21). W 53rd. St. @ 6th. Ave.	75-81 decibels	1104 hrs. Monday.
22). E 55th. St. @ 5th. Ave.	80-83 decibels	1610 hrs. Monday.
23). W 81st. St. @ Columbus Circle	80-91 decibels*	0930 hrs. Tuesday.
24). W 38th. St. @ 9th. Ave.	89-92 decibels*	1015 hrs. Tuesday.
25). E 42nd. St. @ Madison	84 decibels	1045 hrs. Tuesday.
26). E 75th. St. @ Madison	78-84 decibels	1108 hrs. Tuesday.
27). E 82nd. St. @ 5th. Ave. (Met. Museum fountain)	86 decibels	1356 hrs. Tuesday.
28). E 51. St. @ 5th. Ave.	86-91 decibels*	1705 hrs. Tuesday.
29). Watts St. @ W. Boadway	84-96 decibels*	1105 hrs. Wednesday.
30). Canal St. @ Broadway	88-94 decibels*	1124 hrs. Wednesday.
31). Liberty St. @ Greenwich Ave.	80-82 decibels	1343 hrs. Wednesday.

203

32). Wall St. @ Broadway	80-82 decibels	1357 hrs. Wednesday.
33). Vietnam Vets. Mem. Plaza	80-84 decibels	1420 hrs. Wednesday.
34). Battery Park @ Greenwich	81-82 decibels	1451 hrs. Wednesday.
35). Columbus Circle	81-85 decibels	1023 hrs. Thursday.
36). W 56th. St. @ 7th. Ave.	78-94 decibels	1032 hrs. Thursday.
37). Columbus Circle.	78-88 decibels	1612 hrs. Thursday.
38). Grand Army Plaza	84-88 decibels	1642 hrs. Thursday.
39). Columbus Circle.	79-94 decibels*	1210 hrs. Friday.
40). Grand Army Plaza	84-86 decibels	1305 hrs. Friday.

204

Appendix II

Common Noise Levels and Typical Reactions

Sound Source	Noise Level dB	Acceptance Loudness	Typical Reaction	CMHC Requirements		
				Categories	dB	Maximum Acceptable Level
	135	Sixty-Four times as loud	Painfully Loud	Unacceptable		
Military Jets	130		Limit Amplified Speech			
Jet Takeoff at 200'	120	Thirty-two times as loud				
	110	Sixteen times as loud	Maximum vocal effort			
Jet Takeoff at 2000'	100	Eight times as loud				
Freight Train at 50'	95					
Heavy Truck at 50' Busy City Street	90	Four times as loud	Very annoying Hearing damage (8 Hours)			
	80	Twice as loud	Annoying		75	
Highway Traffic at 50'	70	Base Reference	Telephone use difficult	Unacceptable without adequate sound insulation		
	60	Half as loud	Intrusive		55	Outdoor recreation
Light Car Traffic at 50'				Normally Acceptable	45	
Noisy Office	50	Quarter as loud	Speech interference		45	Kitchens Bathrooms
Public Library	40	Eighth as loud	Quiet		40	Living/ Dining
Soft Whispers at 15'	30	Sixteenth as loud	Very Quiet		35	Bedrooms
	10	Sixty-fourth as loud	Just Audible	Acceptable		
Threshold of Hearing	0					

NOTE : The minimum difference in noise level that is noticeable to the human listener is 3 dB. A 10 dB increase in level appears to double the loudness while a 10 dB. decrease halves the apparent loudness.

205

Appendix III

Spark Street Mall, Ottawa

Pedestrian Count.

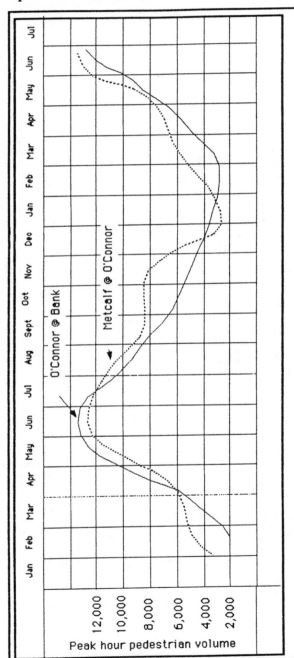

Appendix IV

Canadian Cities.

St John's, Newfoundland.
City Population. 96,216.
City area. 102 sq. km.
Metro population. 161,900.
Provincial economy. Mining, manufacturing, fishing, pulp and paper, electricity production.

Halifax, Nova Scotia.
City Population. 113,577.
City area. 80 sq. km.
Metro population. 296,000.
Provincial economy. Manufacturing, fishing, mining, tourism, agriculture, forestry.

Charlottetown, Prince Edward Island.
City Population. 15,776.
City area. 7 sq. km.
Provincial economy. Agriculture, tourism, fisheries, light manufacturing.

Moncton, New Brunswick.
City Population. 55,468.
City area. 141 sq. km.

Saint John, New Brunswick.
City Population. 76,381.
City area. 323 sq. km.
Metro population. 121,300
Provincial economy. Manufacturing, fishing, mining, forestry, pulp and paper.

Québec, Québec.
City Population. 164,580.
City area. 89 sq. km.
Metro population. 603,300.
Provincial economy. Manufacturing, agriculture, electricity
  production, mining, meat processing, petroleum refining.

Montreal, Québec.
City Population. 1,015,420.
City area. 177 sq. km.
Metro population. 2,921,400

Ottawa, Ontario.
City Population. 300,763.
City area. 110 sq. km.
Metro (Ottawa/Hull) population. 819,300
Provincial economy. Manufacturing, finance, construction,
  tourism, agriculture, forestry.

208

Toronto, Ontario.
City Population. 612,289.
City area. 97 sq. km.
Metro population. 3,427,200.

Winnipeg, Manitoba.
City Population. 594,551.
City area. 572 sq. km.
Metro population. 625,300.
Provincial economy. Manufacturing, agriculture, slaughtering
  and meat processing, mining.

Saskatoon, Saskatchewan.
City Population. 177,641.
City area. 132 sq. km.
Metro population. 200,700

Regina, Saskatchewan.
City Population. 175,064.
City area. 110 sq. km.
Metro population. 186,500.
Provincial economy. Agriculture, mining, meat processing,
  electricity production, petroleum refining.

Edmonton, Alberta.
City Population. 573,982.
City area. 670 sq. km.
Metro population. 785,500.
Provincial economy. Oil production, mining, agriculture, beef
  ranching, manufacturing, construction.

Calgary, Alberta.
City Population. 636,104.
City area. 535 sq. km.
Metro population. 671,300.

Vancouver, British Columbia.
City Population. 431,147.
City area. 113 sq. km.
Metro population. 1,380,800

209

Victoria, British Columbia.
City Population. 66,303.
City area. 19 sq. km.
Metro population. 255,600.
Provincial economy. Forestry, mining, tourism, agriculture,
  fishing, manufacturing.

References

Part I. Art is Dead.

Preface.

Hedman, Richard, and Jaszewski, Andrew. *Fundamentals of Urban Design*. Chicago: Planners Press, 1985.

Lang, Jon T. *Creating Architectural Theory: The Role of the Behavioral Sciences in Environmental Design*. New York: Van Nostrand Reinhold, 1986.

Lynch, Kevin. *Good City Form*. Cambridge: M.I.T. Press, 1984.

Magnusson, W. and Sancton, A., eds. *City Politics in Canada*. Toronto: U. of T. Press, 1983.

Rudolfsky, Bernard. *The Prodigious Builders*. New York: Harcourt, Brace, Jovanovich, 1979.

Sitte, Camille. *The Art of Building a City: City Building According to its Artistic Fundamentals*. Westport, Conn.: Hyperion, 1980 (Reprint of 1943 ed.)

Chapter 1.

Atwood, Margaret. "The City Planners," *The Circle Game*. Toronto: Anansi, 1966.

Baker, Joseph. "There's more sizzle than substance in Safdie's musings." *The Gazette,* Montreal, February 28, 1987.

Charles, Prince of Wales. "Corporation of London's Dinner at the Mansion House." Address to architects and planners, London, December 1987.

Eliot, T. S., "The Hollow Men, A penny or the old guy." In *Selected poems*. London: Faber and Faber Limited, 1954.

Godley, Elizabeth. "Sculptures vandalized," *The Vancouver Sun,* June 10, 1988.

Foikis, Joachim. Self appointed town fool, Vancouver, Summer 1969.

Ruskin, John. *Seven Lamps of Architecture.* London, 1849.

Vanelli, Gino, *When I think about those nights in Montreal,* Montreal. Popular song, 1987.

Chapter 2.

Alexander, Christopher, Neis, Hajos, Anninou, Artemis and King, Ingrid. *A New Theory of Urban Design.* New York: Oxford University Press, 1987.

Kalman, Harold and John Roaf. *Exploring Vancouver.* Vancouver: University of British Columbia Press, 1974.

MacDonald, Norbert. *Distant Neighbours.* Lincoln, Neb: University of Nebraska Press, 1987.

Macpherson, C. B., *The Life and Times of Liberal Democracy.* London: Oxford University Press, 1977.

Marley, Bob and the Wailers. Trenchtown, Jamaica, home of Reggae.

Summerson, Sir John. *Georgian London.* London: MIT Press, 1945.

Sutcliffe, Anthony. *The Autumn of Central Paris.* Montreal: McGill-Queen's Press, 1971.

————. *Towards the Planned City.* Oxford: Basil Blackwell, 1981.

Chapter 3.

Allsopp, Robert. "On trying to make a silk purse from a sow's ear. Trinity Park." *Landscape Architectural Review.* December 1987, pp 5-9.

Ashihara, Yoshinobu. *The Aesthetic Townscape.* (Machinami no bigaku). Tokyo: Iwanami Shoten, 1979.

Kepes, Gyorgy. *Language of Vision.* New York: Theobald, 1944.

McGregor, Gaile. *Wacousta Syndrome.* Toronto: University of Toronto Press, 1985.

Minkowski, Hermann. *Space and Time: The Principles of Relativity.* New York: Dover, 1923.

Moholy-Nagy, Lazlo. *The New Vision.* New York, 1930.

Prigogine, Ilya, and Stengers, Isabelle. *Order out of Chaos.* New York: Bantam, 1984.

Whyte, William H., *The Social Life of Small Urban Spaces.* Washington: The Conservation Society, 1980.

212

Chapter 4.

Kueppers, Harald. *The Basic Law of Color Theory.* Cologne: DuMont Buchverlag, 1978.

Mertins, Detlef, ed. *Metropolitan Mutations, The architecture of emerging public spaces.* RAIC Annual 1. Toronto: Little, Brown and Company (Canada) 1989.

Moholy-Nagy, Lazlo. *Vision in Motion.* Chicago: Theobald, 1947.

Smith, Paul. "Calming the Traffic and Sharing the Street." Plan Canada, 26:4.

Part II. Long Live Art.

Chapter 5.

Berthoud, Roger. "Down by the Henry Moore." *Globe & Mail,* Toronto, October 17, 1987.

Chapter 6.

Jacobs, Jane. *Death and Life of Great American Cities.* New York: Random House, 1961.

Mertins, Detlef, and Shim, Brigitte. "Public Space: the State of the Art." *The Canadian Architect,* May 1988, pp. 25-51.

Chapter 7.

Hofstadter, Douglas R. *Gödel, Escher, Bach: An Eternal Golden Thread.* New York: Vintage, 1980.

Kemble, Roger. "A marvelous achievement." *The Canadian Architect,* June 1981, pp. 14-23.

Markson, Jerome. "Market Square for Market Square Associates." Sketch plans, project no. 8006, Toronto, Jerome Markson, Architects, 1982.

Raynaud, Jean-Pierre. "Place de Paris à Québec et réaménagement de l'ancien marché Finlay" (Phase 1, 1987), Annexe 5, Québec, May 25, 1987.

Schoenauer, Norbert. "Maison Alcan." *The Canadian Architect.* April, 1984, pp. 24-33.

213

Chapter 8.

Aremu, Solomon; Brundrige, Richard; Jeffrey Lowe; Ioannis Ziotas; "CNR East Yards Redevelopment '84: A Show Case of Winnipeg's Past and Future." Winnipeg: Institute of Urban Studies, Report No. 17, University of Winnipeg. 1986.

Barnett, Jonathan. *An Introduction to Urban Design.* New York: Harper & Row, 1982.

du Toit, Roger. "Essay in urban design." *The Canadian Architect.* May 1985, pp 24-31.

Krier, Rob. *Urban Space* (Stadtraum). New York: Rizzoli, 1979.

Sheppard, Burt and Associates, and Arends and Associates. *St. John's Heritage Conservation Area Study.* St. John's, Heritage Canada and Newfoundland Historic Trust, 1976.

Thoreau, Henry David. *Walden, or Life in the Woods.* Concord, Mass., 1854.

214

Appendices.

I. Noise level readings taken by Roger Kemble, 1987-88.

II. Central Mortgage and Housing Corporation. *Road and Rail Noise: Effects on Housing.* Ottawa, National Housing Act 5156, 12/77.

III. The City of Ottawa. "Pedestrian Count." Sparks Street Mall, Ottawa,1987.

IV. *The Canadian World Almanac & Book of Facts.* Toronto: Globe,1989.

Index

217

219

The Author

Roger Kemble has been a practising architect, urban designer and planner for two-score years. As writer and illustrator he exhibits not a little of the originality and temperament of his theatrical ancestors. (Roger Kemble, who died in 1802 was the father of Sarah Kemble who became Mrs. Siddons. The author is a direct descendant of her brother Stephen, manager of the Edinburgh Theatre from 1792 to 1800).

A world traveller, but a resident of Vancouver, Roger Kemble was born in Kingston-upon-Hull, Yorkshire, and was educated in England's oldest public school, St. Peter's, York. He received formal training at the Architectural Institute of British Columbia (1952-56) and studied design, painting and sculpture, concurrently, as a member of Jan Zack's Atelier in Victoria, B.C. (1954-57).

Early practical experience in architecture came in the offices of F.W. Nicols, John Wade, the B.C. Provincial Department of Public Works and Gardner Thornton, Gathe & Associates, all of Vancouver. Since 1960 his private practice has encompassed a wide range of architectural, housing, neighbourhood improvement and urban design projects.

In recent years he has served on a number of distinguished award juries and has himself been the recipient of nearly a score of awards, including a National Award, Canadian Housing Design Council (1964), the Massey Silver Medal (1967), Award of Excellence, Canadian Architecture Yearbook (1981), CMHC Graduate Fellowship (1984), Mellon Scholarship (1987), etc. . . .

For a quarter of a century he has had a close relationship with the University of British Columbia, as lecturer and member of thesis committees in the School of Architecture and as a graduate student in the School of Community and Regional Planning. In 1987 he was invited to do critiques of the schools of architecture at the universities of Laval and Montreal.

Between 1965 and 1986 he contributed regularly to *The Canadian Architect* and over the years he has written for a variety of other professional, trade and metropolitan publications. Kemble's service to the arts, theatre and community organizations has been unabated, beginning with the Community Arts Council of Vancouver (director, 1964-70), the Gallimaufry Theatre Company (director, 1970-71), the Carousel Theatre Company (vice-president, 1980-81), the Vancouver Art Gallery (trustee, 1980-81), Town Wayte Renaissance Music Ensemble (director, 1980-81), the Neighbourhood Services Association of Vancouver (governor, 1975-79).

The Royal Architectural Institute of Canada, the Architectural Institute of B.C., the Canadian Institute of Planners and the Planning Institute of B.C. are among his professional associations. As Academician of the Royal Canadian Academy of Arts, he remains loyal to the artistic side of his versatile nature.